Eber & Wein Publishing's

Who's Who
in American Poetry

John T. Eber Sr.

MANAGING EDITOR

A publication of

Eber & Wein Publishing

Pennsylvania

Who's Who in American Poetry: Vol. 2

Library of Congress
Cataloging in Publication Data

ISBN 978-1-60880-291-3

Proudly manufactured in the United States of America by

Eber & Wein Publishing
Pennsylvania

For Ellen + Brent
Love
Dad -

Who's Who
in American Poetry

GOD POEM

God sent me an e mail last night
"For God's sake (that's me) pass on the word
To those stumble-bum poets to stop
Writing ricky-ticky poems about me
Usually in rhyming couplets
In which they accuse me of being the inspiration
For their insipid slop
Which is so much sewage that
If I were still the vengeful God I once was
I'd consign them all to HELL
I'd send them out into the NIGHT
Or PURGATORY
Or God forbid (that's still me)
To TORONTO
They sound …how should I put it …
WIMPY DIMPY : NAMBY PAMBY
Baby words for baby TWITS
Hey! I'm getting a bad rep
As a fossilized old FART
What did I ever do
To deserve THAT! "

(I'm just the messenger, but I'd say
        He's getting
        Goddamned
            MAD)

A Poem Is a Useless Thing

In this utilitarian world, what use is a poem?
You can't pound nails with it, or build bridges
You can't eat it or drink it, or plant crops with it
Try to extract uranium from it, and it won't even go pop!
Load a gun with it, and it will just block the barrel
You can't drive it around the block or fly it over the ocean
If it were for sale in a junkyard, it would be the last thing to go—
And then you'd be lucky if you even got ten dollars for it
So why spend a lifetime learning to write one
Or spend a career teaching something so impractical?
But then a poem is like a sunset
And a sunset doesn't do anything, either
Drink to me only with thine eyes
There are many kinds of thirst
Can Vincent's paintings razor off an ear
And should they, if they could?
Can great concertos soften the blow of a bomb?
In the scheme of things, though, how useful is a bomb?
So in the end, surround me with poems
Paintings, music, sunsets, the love of a woman
And I would forgo much else the world holds dear
For my treasures are what the world discards
Surround me then with these useless things:
They are all that matter

Jim MacNeill
Meota, SK Canada

Poetry is the hardcopy of my inner and outer worlds. My poetry has been published in both Canada and the USA. I worked my way through university on oil rigs and construction: consummate educational experiences. I became a biologist, working as far North as Lake Athabasca. Later I taught both biology and English at the high school level and at the University of Saskatchewan. I was seconded by the Canadian government to work in Africa. Upon my return, I became a collegiate principal, continuing to lecture part-time at the U of S. One year, I was asked to speak at the NCTE conference in Boston. I also worked briefly as an outside editor for the University of Arizona. .

Eber & Wein Publishing

Author of the Unwritten

Sometimes it seems that our destiny is
written with the winged quills of the night,
just like a shadow is written by the light.
Do we build on history's shadows,
or live as time's cast?
Do we live our future,
or are we merely reciting the past?

Derek Walsh
Sherborn, MA

I would like to thank my family. The sun has risen and set on me many times in my life. Poetry and music has always held me together—that and my family. Without them, I would dwell in the shadow hours forever.

2

The Monster Called Anger

The monster called anger
Ate me long ago
When my heart was barely able to understand
What the feeling was

It rips my other emotions to shreds
Pushes them aside
And makes itself the most noticeable
It makes me spew the hatred in my heart

The monster screams and cries
The hated words that leave my mouth
Will never be regretted
Because they are protection
That saves my heart anguish

The people I meet will never know
The real me
Because of the monster
I call anger

Haley Wynne
Glendive, MT

[Hometown] Glendive, MT; [DOB] September 24, 1996; [Ed] high school student; [Occ] student; [Hobbies] writing, reading, studying history; [GA] being published

I'm just a tomboy who vents through writing. This poem was written at a really tough time in my life when I was being bullied. The only way to protect my heart from the verbal beatings it received from peers was to become angry. I became a loner. Here I am, two years later, loving life and no longer being bullied. To those of you who know the pain of being bullied, stay strong; it will get better.

The Way I Am

Some say it's weird,
some say it's crazy,
some shake their heads,
but I don't care.
I have people that love me
just the way I am.
They outnumber the people,
who want me to change.
I am loud
and I laugh when it's not funny,
but that is because I am loved.
I don't care if some don't like it.
I won't be changed,
all because I'm loved,
just the way I am.

Kara S. Olson
Blaine, MN

[Hometown] Blaine, MN; [DOB] March 31, 1993; [Ed] CMA; [Occ] phlebotomist; [Hobbies] drawing, writing

This is dedicated to those who aren't afraid to be themselves. Also, it is a thank you to everyone who loves the people they know for who they are, not who you want them to be.

Hold On to Hope

The cold it seeps in like the drops into the ground when it rains
The chill it creeps in slowly, icily into my veins
The darkness surrounds revealing nothing but black air
The silence of all sounds is eerie but not one little noise do I dare
The time that has passed I could not tell or see
The aching in my bones makes it feel like eternity
The endless solitude is more than just a product of my mind
The past was a life of light with others until it began to unwind
The others started to disappear and the light faded
The lonely constant night became the world depression created
The lifeless emotions grew worse with no signs of being changed
The torment only continued further and I began to grow deranged
Yet a light is growing in the dark, allowing me to cope
Though small it may be and far away, it is still a ray of hope

Kayla Evans
Wayne, MI

[Hometown] Wayne, MI; [DOB] January 27, 1994; [Ed] nursing student at Wayne State; [Hobbies] reading, swimming; [GA] getting my poems published

I have been writing poetry ever since I was little. I usually wrote little poems for my family, but now I write for myself. I always loved reading poems by Robert Frost; his work was a huge inspiration to me. I try to put in words the beauty I see in the world, or I convey the struggles in life that people are forced to face yet are still able to overcome.

Chemo Bad!

My belly started to hurt.
Each passing day, it hurt more.
I finally got my doctor to listen,
I knew something was wrong.
A CT scan was ordered and came back showing a mass.
Go see the surgeon...
A three-pound tumor was removed:
Cancer
Chemotherapy every three weeks, for four months.
Pick lines and fatigue, lose your hair,
Sick to your stomach and chemo brain, words are jumbled.
Wheel chairs and walkers, days in bed until you hate it.
Finally, the sixth and last chemo...
Pick line gone, it's over.
I made it through, and so did my Sweetheart.
Chemo bad!
But without it...
Dead.

Carolyn Isgrig
Las Vegas, NV

[Hometown] Okeene, OK; [DOB] April 21, 1939; [Ed] College of Southern Nevada; [Occ] retired accountant; [Hobbies] crochet; [GA] my three sons

I am a retired accountant and active writer. I enjoy writing—mostly non-fiction short stories. In the last year and a half, I started writing poetry; to my sheer delight, I have been published! I have three sons, all of whom are loving and kind grown men that I am very proud of, and I have been married to my sweetheart for thirty-two years. I attended the College of Southern Nevada for my accounting degree and writing classes (taught by Bob Cawley). I wrote "Chemo Bad" after going through ovarian cancer surgery last year and four long months of chemotherapy.

Wounded Bird

Like a wounded bird
You left me lying in the road,
never knowing how high I soared.

You will never know how hard I fell
how hard I hit the ground
or how injured I lie
here on the road.

Lying here with a broken spirit
and a crack in my heart,
never my story will be told.

You never cared for the bird
high in the tree—a symbol of *me*.

Never heard my song I sung way up high.
Never did you see me fly by and look at you.
I am the bird you ignore and pretend you never knew.
How could you?!

Olga A. Williams
Tamaqua, PA

I am a poet, model, and actress. I love to read and write poetry. My poems are feelings written on paper and a poem is created.

Tone Up on Tuesday

O how we hate to get up in the morning
We rub our eyes and end our snoring.
It is Tuesday now, the time is here.
Only a tone-up, nothing to fear

We get in the Pontiac, it's a '93
There is a parking place there, I see.
We go into the building and arrange a few chairs
We see our friends, some are in pairs.

Stefanie is there controlling this space
The Circle of Care called Leeza's Place
After some healthy deep breaths, our mantra we state
Energize, empower and educate

Irma arrives and we are ready to start
She begins with the philosophical part
Stretches are easy at first, soon the muscles are sore
You think, you can't do them, then there are more

Exercises from China and India and everywhere it seems
Dance steps we do, I haven't done since my teens
The songs at the end, I really like the best
It is chance to give the body a rest.
Finally, they all say, *You have made their day*

Marvin Matlin
Sherman Oaks, CA

Poetry is an unlikely avocation for a CPA. Friends and relatives had urged me to write poems for their festive occasions. I even wrote one for my eightieth birthday, a eulogy for a memorial, and "Birth of Our Art" for a Chicano art exhibit. I wrote "A Caregiver's Reward" about my wife's care. Now, I write mostly poems about holidays: Fourth of July, Rosh Hashana, Valentine's Day, Chanukah and Thanksgiving. For New Year, I told how the holiday is celebrated in other countries. "Tone Up on Tuesday" was about an exercise class in a senior center (Leeza's Place).

Reflection of the Past

What do I see?
A human...
a person...
is that me?
The water goes on
so smooth and vast.
But who's to say
it will last?
What if a great destruction
is coming our way?
We have to hold the peace,
so come and stay.
How do we know
if it will last?
We look back
at the reflection
of the past.
If we stay
with the light,
we will have
no fright.
Our bond will set
powerful rays
to the everlasting
Earth's gaze.
And peace will reign forevermore.

Kristen N. Gallo
Odessa, FL

[Hometown] Tampa, FL; [DOB] December 9, 1999; [Ed] Walker Middle Magnet; [Occ] student, writer; [Hobbies] writing, short stories, poetry, making movies; [GA] winning multiple writing awards before the age of thirteen

I live in Florida with my twin brother and sister; I am a triplet. We are very close. I'm thirteen years old and have a munchkin cat named Wally and a dog named Black Jack. I enjoy living in Florida, except for the fact that it doesn't snow here. Caring about the earth inspires my poetry and helps me with my imagery. One of the main reasons I write is to please God, and that's what matters most to me.

Happy Hunting

I hunt people
Because they are mad.
I hunt people
Because they are bad.
I hunt people
To make others safer.
I hunt people
To make our world a better place to live.
I am hunting to let you know
That our lives are
Most of the time all about choices:
good, bad, sometimes very sad,
But each of them
Gave us a learning lesson,
Doesn't matter which one we are going to have.
Every time we are getting
stronger, wiser and caution too,
As long as we listen to ourselves,
Those experience won't be forgotten.
Those experiences will be ...

Buildin' our character for rest of our lives.

Edyta G. Lapinski
New Britain, CT

[Hometown] Poland; [DOB] October, 19, 1974; [Ed] medical office administration; [Occ] I'm disabled and volunteer in an office and hospital; [Hobbies] paint portraits in acrylic, sketch in pencil; [GA] being in a poetry book Best Poets and Poems of 2012 on first page

I moved from Poland twenty-six years ago because of my epilepsy. I have a lot of hobbies, but since in my family there was a painter, Julian Falat, I share his interest, and I am an artist too. Although my heart and soul is more likely to do poetry, where I can press every button on any kind of subject. My accomplishments include being published in fifteen separate books of poetry, with others that include three international publications and five publications recorded on CD. I received five Editor's Choice Awards. I have my own book of poetry, Fantasy Island, published by Xlibris. "Happy Hunting" was written based on my favorite show Criminal Minds, where the FBI hunts down the worst kind of criminals by doing their profiles. That's why the title is "Happy Hunting."

The Colors You Give Me

I have painted pictures of our love in poetry
By way of colors found among words you spoke
Your expressions fill my palette with shades opaque
Your whispers propose depth with every brush stroke
Perception of feelings, the emanations of your eyes
Are paintable with the sound of my lyric's voice
Glistening emotions from your spirit of affection
Becomes hues of your motley heart's ardent choice
Imbued language your body speaks as we commune
Is as vivid as the radiance in a double rainbow
Thus containment to my canvas size suffers want
As the abundance of words from my page overflow
So brilliant are the colors of who you are
I would know you not if it weren't for these
They speak of your soul and of your worth
More than polished demands, your facets do please
The colors you give me suffuse as we linger
Merging into an appearance that's most unique of all
Adoringly I capture that scene of your splendid glow
In an elegant masterpiece upon my heart's wall
Modestly you back away from what I say
Your humility shy from what I see you be
Yet I'm inclined to paint you in an honest reflection
For I paint precisely the colors you give me

Dick R. Cullen
Apopka, FL

[Hometown] Sandusky, OH; [DOB] January 3, 1945; [Ed] high school; [Occ] finish carpentry; [Hobbies] collecting antique cookware, cooking, writing; [GA] raising a family that I enjoy

I am a father of four and have been a finish carpenter most of my life. Now, I am retired. I make a habit of writing true-life happening—some of my own life, but usually the life of others which in some way involve or affect me. Experiences of real life are the events which hold the most feeling, passion, excitement and usually all future meaning to a person. The capturing of these moments in written form along with the understanding of oneself holds the key to most other situations that will be faced, especially those that demand decision-making.

The Exonerator

First of his kind elected to such a position
He never tires while doing good
He knows that the deserved will reap the reward
Uncertain of what his labors will produce
He merely strives for truth with a heart bent on justice
He occupies a position of high rank
A hero to those who know him well
His heart a moral compass, a soul guided by social duty
Ever achieving and pursuing justice
Conqueror of tyranny, slayer of injustice.
He knows that liberty lies in the heart and not in the cold law.
Each day is marked by intellect and elegance.
In the courtroom he strives valiantly for the worthy cause
And conquers injustice along with a plethora of experts in every filed
Calm, serene, sublime in the knowledge that freedom is the reward.
His true adversary is simply injustice.
History will be the final judge of his work.
The exonerations, a legal footprint on the sands of time.

Cindy Stormer
Dallas, TX

[Hometown] Gainsville, TX; [DOB] May 22, 1956; [Ed] attorney, juris doctorate; [Occ] attorney; [Hobbies] classical guitar; [GA] exoneration of wrongfully accused

Cindy Stormer is an assistant district attorney for the Dallas district attorney's office. She was the DNA attorney when Dallas was experiencing unprecedented numbers of exonerations of wrongfully convicted individuals. She investigated and re-evaluated hundreds of cases to determine if there were wrongfully convicted persons in Texas prisons, with a special emphasis on DNA. She appeared in a documentary in real time, Dallas DNA, which has aired on the Investigation Discovery Channel and others since 2009. She is the author of Texas Small Firm Practice Tools (by James Publishing), a law book covering sixteen practice areas.

Eternal Flame of Hope

One candle cannot burn all day,
One heart, one mind—will not exist forever.
But if love is introduced to the pair,
Then hope will surely not despair.

Death creeps in at every waking moment,
Life blinds thee to the point of insanity.
But if love is introduced to the pair,
Then hope will surely not despair.

If love breeds hope, then hope breeds life,
And the fetter which binds one's soul together
Can be broken by the flame of hope,
This burns the candles of life and love.

For the two souls of life and death are
More often than not immensely distraught,
But the shackles of despair and pain
Can be broken by the flame of hope.

And if that flame burns throughout,
Then love and hope will coexist, no doubt.
Because death will shatter,
And life will matter.

Annelda Michelle Morris
Cleburne, TX

[Hometown] Cleburne, TX; [DOB] November 25, 1986; [Ed] college graduate; [Hobbies] playing the fiddle, writing, acting, singing; [GA] overcoming adversity

I've been through a lot in my life, more than any twenty seven-year-old should—throughout my education, participating in my college choir, playing my fiddle, and life experiences. Regardless of my busy life, I still found time to write over two hundred poems and a few stories. I wrote this poem when I got out of the hospital from my third brain surgery at the age of seventeen. The experience made me realize hope and love can never be lost, broken or shattered, no matter how great the adversity, because the fire of hope and love comes from within.

My Friend

Your phone calls have become a lifeline to me,
You are like the air that I breathe.
You help me get through the very next day,
It's really hard to know what to say.
I can't see what you see in me
Or why you want to be my friend
I wait all day with phone near by,
Just to hear you talk and laugh or text on the fly.
But you're what keeps me going every day.
The fear that this might end is weighing heavy on my mind,
So for now I will stay by the phone until it is time,
thoughts of the other are too dark and no life at all,
will I stand or will I fall?

Tonja L. Wright
Las Vegas, NV

[Hometown] Nashville, IN; [DOB] February 26, 1953; [Ed] BA in scenic design; [Occ] disabled; [Hobbies] reading, writing, painting; [GA] becoming a human being, everything I have learned from Irena and Yosef Geshuri

I live in Las Vegas, but my heart is in Brown County, IN. A friend of my brother's became my friend forty years ago, and now he is a great friend to me. Great friends are hard to find. I have found three: Irera and Yosef Geshuri have been there for me, and Darryl talks to me every day. I want to thank all three of you for being in my life.

Welcome Home Gilad Shalit

Gilad, Gilad, you never
gave up hope,
Nor faith in the mercy
of Ha Shem.

Few will ever know
the physical, mental
and emotional pain
you suffered,
During 1941 days
of unjust incarceration!

And we, your brothers
and sisters; "Children
of the Book,"
Never gave up hope
either.

And I for one, as a veteran
of the war in Southeast Asia,
Want to say what my
country took twenty years to say
to me:
Welcome home my brother;
Welcome home brave son!

Jefferson Murphy
Milton, NY

[Hometown] Milton, NY; [DOB] August 25, 1947; [Ed] two years college; [Occ] general contractor; [Hobbies] art, music, books; [GA] being a husband and father

For fifty-three years I have blessed Israel the land and Israel the people. As a Vietnam vet, I hate war and am in sympathy for anyone who must fight in them. Gilad Shalit was kidnapped and tortured for nearly five years. No one cares more for one life than Israel. There are no finer soldiers on Earth than the Israel Defense Force.

My Papa

My Papa John is a handyman,
He can fix just about anything,
He isn't just any type of handyman, he can cook too.
My Papa makes the best Reubens in the whole world and nobody can duplicate them,
He always helps people out even if you tell him not to, he cares about everyone even if he
doesn't know you, Papa does know more than anybody I know.
My Papa often hurts from all the hard work he does but he still finds time to be with his
grandchildren, children, and friends. He always encourages people to do their best and he
doesn't get too upset when we leave his house a complete mess
Papa is clever, hardworking and solicitous
So let's all gather around because we are so privileged to have a man like Papa John in our lives.

Alexandra Weir
Van Meter, IA

*I am a junior at Van Meter High School in Van Meter, IA. I live with my mom, stepdad, and four siblings.
Some of my hobbies include playing bass guitar, writing poetry, working with children who have special needs,
and spending time with my family. I wrote this poem for my Papa John because he has always been there
for me.*

Nightmare

I'm lying outside on the cool, green grass
Looking up at the bright, blue sky
And white, fluffy clouds
I close my eyes, and memories flash through my mind
It's like I'm in a nightmare
I sit up, and the sky has darkened
To pitch-black darkness
No sun or clouds
I can't see anything around me
I'm on my feet, running
Trying to run from my past
My heart catches on fire
It burns as it goes through all the breaks
Made by those whom I love
Now I see blood dripping down the darkness
As if they were walls
I trip and fall, I can't get back up
My body, so numb as tears fall down my face
Closing my eyes for a second
I sit up, rubbing my eyes
Blue sky and green grass around me
My tears—really raindrops, as it starts to lightly rain

Jessica N. Rodrigues
Moorhead, IA

[Hometown] Moorhead, IA; [DOB] January 20, 1994; [Ed] college sophomore, studying nursing; [Occ] CNA, sales associate; [Hobbies] reading, writing, music; [GA] having my poetry published

I was born and raised in Tulare, CA. In 2007, I moved to Iowa. I am the youngest of three children. My poetry is inspired by my own personal experiences and emotions. Some of my poems are a little dark, but so is my past. My life is getting better, and my poems are getting lighter. I now live in Moorhead, IA with my wonderful boyfriend who supports me always, along with my loving parents. I'm going to college for nursing and hope to help those in need. I love nature, the outdoors and animals.

Self-Inflicted

People judge her.
"She's so skinny."
"Too short."
"Not good enough."
"Plain."
"Too quiet."
They don't know they're hurting her.

Her bright eyes fade.
Her smile dies and turns into a fake.
She acts invincible,
But she is just invisible.

She returns home and locks herself away,
Escaping the world with music,
Dreading tomorrow,
Wanting to do it all over,
To change.

She wants to change,
So she writes and writes...
But there are no pens and pencils...
All there is are knives and razors.
And her body is the canvas,
For all her self-inflicted hate.

Mikaela Nikole Myers
Chesapeake, VA

[Hometown] Carrsville, VA; [DOB] April 23, 1996; [Ed] senior high school; [Hobbies] writing, reading; [GA] getting four poems published

God Is Faithful

Surely goodness and mercy
Have attended our way,
As we recount the past,
His promises never failed us;
To them we did hold fast.
I've learned as the years roll onward,
To leave the past behind.
That's what the Father told us
If true contentment we'd find.
The disappointments, trials, and tests
We found were for our good.
For God gives to His children
Only that which is for the best.
As we stand at the portal of the opening year
Not knowing what it holds,
We once again have His promises
As each new day unfolds.
His comfort, strength, encouragement
Will be ours each step of the way,
As we continue in the Word
And as we watch and pray.
He'll never fail us nor forsake,
So what do we have to fear?
We serve an all-sufficient God
Who's more than enough for the coming year!

Margaret R. Smith
Hobe Sound, FL

[Hometown] Hobe Sound, FL; [DOB] May 1, 1929; [Ed] high school graduate; [Occ] ch. sec. treas., doctor's office; [Hobbies] crafts, puzzle, writing, fishing; [GA] published author of 366 daily devotional

I am an eighty-four-year-old widow of about two years now, with three children, six grandchildren and three great-grandsons. For many years now, God inspired me at various times to put poetic form to the thoughts and impressions in my heart that He gave me on a variety of topics and occasions. It is only through divine inspiration that this can be done, so I gratefully acknowledge this gift from my Father. My prayer is that all who read this will be greatly strengthened and encouraged on the journey of life.

In-Sync

Smiles are natural and bright,
not forced to be polite.
Eyes sparkle with the glint of care,
not the dullness of distance or beware.

Touch harmonizes vibrations flowing though,
not pulse-less contact suggesting, "I tolerate you!"
Voices are gentle, soothing, giddy, or direct,
not grating, shrill or full of disrespect.

Ideas and notions tag on, one to the other,
not over, below, or through, like "Why bother."
Interests and desires may differ, but not antagonize,
not fall by the wayside, with a refusal to recognize.

Conversation is a tapestry of joy, comfort, and "we."
not halting, pregnant silences, or "me."
Goals and objectives find support and guidance,
not chagrin, mockery, or diplomatic avoidance.

In-sync is when an exchanged look gives you a thrill,
when footprints and heartbeats mesh to a common will.
In-sync is when what you do is comfortable and right,
when productive days pulse gently into peaceful nights.

Ronald M. Ruble
Huron, OH

*[Hometown] Huron, OH; [DOB] July 4, 1940; [Ed] PhD in Theatre; [Occ] retired college professor;
[Hobbies] creative writing: poetry, prose, plays; [GA] my sons, Eric and Kris*

*I am an associate professor emeritus of humanities at Firelands College of Bowling Green State University.
I have two sons and six grandchildren. I am an award winning playwright and have earned national and
international awards as a poet and fiction writer. I have authored two books, The Pulse of Life, and Words
Walk. I believe we all have lives full of extraordinary moments. The process of living, while diverse and
different per person, is our bond of humanity. I try to capture moments; to look at one thing, but see another.
"In-Sync" captures such moments.*

Blue Love Lights…

Where a soft breeze sways from side to side
supple willow braids slowly shake,
the night silence dropped sky stars so bright
in a motionless darkened lake.
It seems, simply by themselves only,
such mysterious summer nights,
under the water blaze up lonely
at the bottom, blue eyes of lights.

And as if in those night lakes, my dear,
I peer in your mischievous eyes.
What's in them? My flame shines, or appear,
blue lights of your fondness so nice?
Maybe suddenly some wind will burst,
our days will be replaced by nights,
tempests will spring up, thick and too fast—
will grow dim, these blue cheerful lights.

There where the wind swings from side to side
willow braids without any break,
the night silence dropped far stars so bright
in a motionless dormant lake.
Our luck's not in a calm—let the rout,
hurricane, storms, and any fights,
if only they would never go out,
these adorable blue love lights.

Leonid Vaysman
Los Angeles, CA

[Hometown] Kiev, the Ukraine; [DOB] September 13, 1932; [Ed] PhD; [Occ] retired; [Hobbies] poetry

Primal Instinct

It's dark and you can't see a thing
Heartbeat quickens as fear kicks in
Voices and sounds carried on the wind
The panic sets in as you prepare
It's the fight or flight moment
You stand your ground
Bravery trumps fear this time
Silly bravery powered by stubbornness
The refusal to stand down
No matter the odds
Taken in stride
While they stalk their prey
The prey prepares for this fight
Adrenaline at the ready
The fight for life is all that matters
A doubt will not enter
Death is not an option
Don't worry now
Just fight
Just win
Your life is at stake

Sara Litteral
Keansburg, NJ

[Hometown] Keansburg, NJ; [DOB] August 15, 1993; [Ed] AA by December; [Occ] cashier; [Hobbies] art, music, and writing

Hurt

I looked back at yesterday and saw my mistakes,
Full of wrong choices and plenty of heartaches.

I wondered why my choices had been so wrong,
Who could I ask to help me along?

I fell to my knees and held my hands in prayer,
I cried out, dear God, are You there?

A warm light filled my being to place me at ease,
It was the Spirit of God that had come to please.

As the time passed inexorably slow,
I failed to the progress I had hoped I would grow.

His omnificent greatness filled my head,
"You have not the humbleness to go where my Son tread."

"Once you die to self and worldly desire,
You will grow to be spiritually inspired."

"You must abandon the gods of possession,
And seek me out for intercession."

"My greatest desire is to fill your heart,
And guide you to freedom once you do your part,"

This lamentable story is not near completion,
I have mountains to climb and His strength not to weaken.

James Garrett Jr.
El Reno, OK

[Hometown] El Reno, OK; [DOB] January 8, 1944; [Ed] high school, electrical tech school; [Occ] semi-retired, Ebay sales; [Hobbies] website design, computers; [GA] getting a job with a major computer company as a field service engineer

My mother loved to write poetry; she saw beauty in the sublime things of life, and her poems were of a sad but spiritual nature, as are mine. I like to take the reader down a road of his own imagination, leaving him to a conclusion of his own. I believe in a multi-dimensional world with curtains of a hidden realm that prevents us from seeing all. Therefore, we must steer a voyage that leads us eventually to the eternal life where we are free from pain and experience joy!

Remission Your Sins

No matter how many times we fall and stumble
Down the path we choose to take
Even if our worlds start to crumble
We cannot allow ourselves to break
Because in life, we will struggle
With our own decisions, mistakes, and shortcomings
Life seems to be nothing but a complicated puzzle
That's incomplete and missing pieces leaving openings
To shelter frustration and doubt that causes hesitation and trouble
But you need to lift yourself off of your knees to which you fell defeated
Lift your head up and fill yourself with determination
Keep your mind wide open to everything and give your all where it is needed
Let your emotions be set free and drive you forward
Let go and scream to demand order
Fight for what you believe in, no matter the torture
Lift your palms up, and protest the ones who don't care
Dare to be different and make them aware
That you are here to stay through the struggle and fight
No matter the tears shed, the mouths full of hate, or what has been
Be prepared to remission your sins
For everyone is called before a judge to take responsibility
Whether it be a god or your heart, it can't be escaped
Not ever through the ties of infinity

Georgia Sroka
Decherd, TN

"No one can tell you who you are." "I believe that we all fall down sometimes." Both these quotes are from a favorite band of mine. They are both true. No one can tell you who you are and we all do fall down sometimes. That's how I got started with my poetry. I fell down and used poetry to build me back up. We all need something to build us up. I found mine; music and writing.

If I Look Up at the Stars

If I look up at the stars
I find myself looking at Heaven.
I only want to find your star.
So I can blow you one last kiss.
So I can give you one more hug.
So I can tell you what has happened since you have been gone.
So I can feel whole again.
So I won't feel the pain anymore.
So I won't feel alone again.
So I won't cry any longer.
So I won't have to hide.
So you can wipe away my tears.
So you can tell me you love me, and I to you.
So you can make it better.
So you can protect me like you always did.
If I look up at the stars
I find myself wishing you were here.

Josephine Cabrera
Glendale, AZ

[Hometown] *Glendale, AZ;* [DOB] *January 10, 1997;* [Ed] *high school sophomore student;* [Hobbies] *guitar, writing, theater;* [GA] *keeping a 4.0 GPA last year*

My first poem, "What Is Faith," came out over three years ago. "If I Look Up at the Stars" is my sixth published poem. My poems have been the work of my past. My father died in October 2009, and since, I have grown physically, mentally and spiritually. In this poem, we learn of a "person" who misses someone and feels their presence at night. This was a midnight poem that brings me to tears whenever I read it because I can still feel the hurt in me when I wrote it. This is for those who need it.

need

winter seeds' diapason
soaring at night
in temperance of trees
to superscription
in reliquary of lights
with its baton
advancing syntax
of forever rising glee
in bread
of the angels' town
releases view
of mansions and raptors
in shining shadows
looming loud
in their length
silent and still,
finally the raptor
with lens perfection
in surveyor's eye
sets the point
and talons thrive
off on wing
in argosy of glory,
and long the mansion
remains insouciant
still and smug

Michael Kirby Smith
Baltimore, MD

[Hometown] Baltimore, MD; [Ed] bachelor's degree; [Occ] land surveyor; [Hobbies] soccer; [GA] two children

Michael K. Smith was born in Ann Arbor, grew up in the country fifteen miles north thereof and was further nourished by the Quaker faith. Six months after being conferred a bachelor of arts degree by Albion College, he was inspired by Thoreau to become a land surveyor and is so registered professionally in Maryland, where he has been a sole proprietor since 1988. Michael resides in Baltimore with his bride of thirty-three years, Mary T. Keating, his daughter Cailin (seventeen) and his son Kirby (fifteen).

Uncharted Cupid Enchanted Islands

The endless truth of your love filled with
romance grains of sand from the
deep blue island of passion shores,
I found hidden in cupid's bottles
in the form of love letters and lost notes.
The currents of the mysteriously colored
waters swept it to shore one day.
When I read it, it cast a spell on my
heart, swept my worries away.
Under the glistening green palm trees,
Cupid set them to sail through the
misty oceans on tiny boats that
pirates seek adventures on. Here they
come! Hear our love soaring through the
aqua colored shores. For every time
I embrace them for love, and for everything
in between. For your love all my
strength I save.

Gohar Minassian
Los Angeles, CA

[Hometown] Hollywood; [DOB] June 24, 1989; [Ed] Art Institute, animation and design; [Occ] layout designer; [Hobbies] drawing, painting, sculpting; [GA] 2008 Congressional Award Gold Medalist

I became inspired to write this poem when I saw a Rococo painting of cupids. I have four medals from the U.S. Congress, which I am so thankful for. I have a very blessed life.

Light Up the Moon

Light up the moon,
Like the evening stars.
Light up the moon,
Like a sweet new car.
Light up the moon,
Like the 4th of July.
Light up the moon,
Like sweet moon pie.
Light up the moon,
Like a sweet tune.
Light up the moon,
Like a new moon.

Laura Hoeppner
Aurora, CO

*[Hometown] Aurora, CO; [Ed] high school; [Occ] student; [Hobbies] drawing, reading;
[GA] art displayed*

Mother's Legacy

She taught me to treat everyone as an equal and stand among
others proud of who and what I am.
She showed me how to be kind to God's creatures and that
love is the ultimate respect.

She impressed on me to avoid trouble, but to stand my
ground when pressed.
She encouraged me to hold strong to my beliefs,
to plant my feel on higher morals.

She told me my arms are for reaching out to those in need, not
pushing away those God put in my path for good reason.
She said friend or foe, I need to be big enough in heart to help,
and to never step down to a lower plane by walking away.

She gave me the knowledge of how to lend a helping hand,
yet not make people feel like they are taking charity.
She guided me to open my mind and heart, to do what I
can to make this a better world.

She still lives today, I can thankfully say, another gift
in and of itself.
She can see what I've done with the wisdom she gave me,
and feel pride, because she awoke the human in me.

Sherry Creswell
Dallas, OR

*[Hometown] Cottonwood, ID; [DOB] September 12, 1953; [Ed] two years college; [Occ] writer; [Hobbies]
painting, drawing, jewelry making; [GA] having my poetry published*

The Tongue

The tongue is a two-edged sword
as told by our Lord.

Degrading someone is a sin.
It hurts way down within.

Don't just be nice and polite to strangers and friends.
Remember your kin.

How do you teach table manners
if you never sit at the table?

Be kind, considerate, thankful whenever you are able.
You will feel good and so will they.

When should we start?
How about today.

Martha M. Porter
Blairsville, GA

[Hometown] Mansfield, OH; [DOB] August 7, 1924; [Ed] graduate of Mansfield Senior High; [Occ] retired; [Hobbies] painting, sewing, crocheting; [GA] being a mother, grandma, and great-grandmother

Every Time

Life,
Life is far from what it seems
Every day is a new beginning

Each day I wake and look
to the skies asking one thing

A heart of gold and strength
to pursue my dreams

Each morning I remember
days are short
Remembering what's important

Each night I sleep I dream
I dream of a different life

I dream of a day when
I'll see you next to me
again…

Each day I remember all the times
we had together all the laughs
we shared together.

Mikayla Cyphert
Mount Pleasant, MI

[Hometown] Mount Pleasant, MI; [DOB] February 5, 1995; [Ed] high school; [Hobbies] writing, painting; [GA] being published

One More Fighting Chance

I was born with gypsy blood is what they say,
never wanting to settle down.
When the scenery got boring to me,
I just picked up and found a new town.
I ran from good relationships, jobs and friends.
I was warned, someday, your roaming must come to an end.
I have risen a new day in Buzzards Bay
Stayed in the southwest desert to watch the setting sun.
Yet all the homes I have had through the years,
I have never owned a single one.
Now, I see the lines of age beginning on my face
My heart is whispering, stay in one place.
So on my knees I start to pray,
Lord, just one more fighting chance, that's all I need.
This time, Lord, I will let you lead.
I followed my heart to the Sunshine State,
where I met a man who became my mate.
We married and bought a Mountain home,
I promised him, on God's word, I would never roam.
I can thank God for my answered prayer.
I let go, and He showed me He cares.
Lord, just one more fighting chance is what people need.
If only they would learn to let You lead.

Deanna Stephens
Morganton, NC

I am now fifty-seven years old. I reside with my husband and three pets near the Blue Ridge Mountain Parkway. I have been writing poetry since I was sixteen. Since I became a Christian, my writings have become more inspirational and a testimony of things I have seen and been through in my life.

Convergences and Paradox: Rambling Thoughts

… for science art and theology to exist on a like plane
is to tease with the curious and to flirt with the insane
so when Einstein, Frost and Christ sang a like refrain
disquisition trumped the paradox and converged
                              "a whole new game"
as relativity with its activity eliminates the mass
then infinite energy equals infinite speed and love
                              "dominates, alas"
for in "the theory relative" speed intimates with age
and so with "big bang centers" love forever sets the stage

now bring forth the poet "Frost" with poem "The Masters Speed"
for it is a place for couples to dwell, forever, yes indeed!

      remiss if i am not to mention
      that we live a new dimension
      great minds have given us the urge
      that speed and age and love converge …

James V. Waldron
San Jose, CA

Our Secret

Come a little closer,
Babe, come a little closer—
Let me whisper in your ear.
Let me tell you softly,
So that nobody else will hear.
What I have to say is private,
And just between us two;
I just want you to know how much
I love the things you do.

I will always love you, babe.
You are my one and only.
I love you with all my heart and soul.

Christa Milby
Aurora, CO

[Hometown] Aurora, CO; [DOB] June 1993; [Ed] college graduate, BA in speech communication; [Hobbies] cruising with my son, traveling; [GA] earning my BA from University of Denver

I live in Aurora, CO with my son, Ian. Ian was the one who encouraged me to write poetry. I love writing poetry in my spare time. Look for more to come!

Dad

Dad, you and Mom are the reason I'm here
You both protect my eyes from a tear
Dad, I love the way I always have your support
Because of you, I have become a great sport
Dad, I know I'll always have your love and care
Daughters and dads always make a great pair
Dad, nothing will ever keep us apart
You truly hold a special place in my heart
Dad, I will cherish all our special moments
I love the looks I get from you with my comments
Dad I will always see you as a friend
I hope we are together in the end

Raven J. Goodman
Glenwood, IA

[Hometown] Glenwood, IA; [DOB] July 1, 1984; [Hobbies] drawing pictures, collecting Reba McEntire and Michael Jordan things

I sit at home and create my own graphic designs without computers. I can't work, because I have epilepsy; I have had it for sixteen years. I'm glad God gave these seizures to me instead of someone else—it has made me who I am. I collect Reba McEntire things, because her songs uplift my spirits. I also collect Michael Jordan memorabilia. My doctors are making me have brain surgery to try and stop my epilepsy. I prefer to help others before helping myself. I write poetry to release my feelings before it's too late. I'm proud to be a Mormon and a poet.

Wild Place

In this wild place,
hearts beat together.
Magic in the rhythm,
solace in the space.

In this wild place
I've found the reason,
already know the answer...
I touch my dream.

In this wild place,
I'm no longer alone.
Vast expanse is ours,
to see and discover.

In this wild place,
time is the turning wheel—
we spin too.

Darla D. Green
Glade Park, CO

[Hometown] Grand Junction, CO; [DOB] May 29, 1960; [Ed] Colorado Mesa University; [Occ] early intervention case manager; [Hobbies] jewelry making, photography, and hiking; [GA] helping children with special needs to attain independence and reach their full potential

I've always had a special place in my heart for the desert and its vast beauty. Growing up in western Colorado, I was fortunate enough to spend a great deal of my childhood exploring these wild spaces. Now, as an adult, I also have the great fortune of living on forty acres of the very desert places I spent time as a child. This poem is a reflection of the appreciation I feel for these wonderful, and breathtakingly beautiful wild places.

Cries in the Sky

My glorious flag
Fluttered in the breeze
Our eagle eyes
Cried in the skies
This proud banner
Delivers war cries
Of an unspeakable death
That extinguished their last breath
All-consuming heat
Igniting fuel
Engulfed their torsos
Calculating, brutal, cruel.

So they flew
Like fleeing doves
On the waves of the wind
Blowing from within
To their own end
To their freedom
To savor safety
With God Almighty

So now I see
My flag unfurled
And weep for their souls
Who tragically left our world.

Hallette C. Dawson
Herndon, VA

[Hometown] Atlanta, GA; [DOB] July 22, 1947; [Ed] Frankfurt High School and Schillar College; [Hobbies] reading, crafting, antiques

I am a sixty-six-year-old homemaker. I live alone with my cat, Millie. I have a twenty-six-year-old daughter who is getting married this coming September; she lives down south. I have always loved poetry, and I have been writing since high school. My mother bought me an anthology when I was a child with authors such as Robert Frost, Walt Whitman and Longfellow. I love to just sit for hours and read their poetry. I have won a few awards for my poems, and I have been published since 1990. I've published with the International Poetry Hall of Fame and Quill Books. I am also a member of the Famous Poets Society.

With You

To see the sun in your eyes,
to hear beauty in your voice,
listening to your laugh
is what I get when I'm with you.

Seeing how gentle you are,
knowing how much you care,
to feel your lips on my neck
is what I get when I'm with you.

Excited to see your face,
overjoyed just to hug you,
wanting to hold you close
is what I get when I'm with you.

Briana Boggio
Great Falls, MT

[Hometown] *Bridger, MT;* [DOB] *January 14, 1987;* [Ed] *high school graduate;* [Occ] *Air Force and National Guard;* [Hobbies] *writing poems and artwork;* [GA] *when I joined the military*

I am Briana Boggio and I grew up in Bridger, MT. I have a twin brother, an older brother, and an older sister. My family and friends inspire me and make me happy. This poem is dedicated to Kacey Power. I hope he sees how happy he makes me. My parents are always there for me and I thank them. I am the youngest in the family and I am twenty-six years old. I plan on one day publishing my own book of my poems.

Formal Education

The fourteen-year-old is pregnant
That ten-year-old can't read...
Though they still stand by, stringent
By their practiced broken creed.

Do I really have to go back?
The teacher got arrested.
That boy got in trouble, because he's black...
No one even protested.

"You'll never amount to anything!"
Learning to just numb, ignore.
As much as you pretend, everything,
It hurts down to the core.

This child doesn't know the color wheel
I just can't help but cry.
I'm here, can't find the words to feel;
I think I found the reason why.

Courtney L. Nay
Shinnston, WV

[Hometown] Adamsville, WV; [DOB] May 16, 1991; [Ed] BS in history from FSU, graduated cum laude; [Occ] market research, amateur writer; [Hobbies] video games, reading; [GA] earning scholarships and graduating from college

I would not be where I am now if it were not for some of the teachers who inspired me. I definitely would not be a poet if it were not for my poetry professor in college. I am so thankful for these amazing people who helped me so much. However, I often feel I am successful in spite of my education, rather than because of it. This poem was fueled by all the hardships I experienced while going through public school, as well as the problems I see children experiencing now.

Heaven's Sacred Strain

In the echo chamber of silence
Where lips are often sealed
Fear seizes mind's eye
And the heart stirs in disbelief
While darkness spins, illusions cry
An angelic choir raises voices
In cantus and sacred harmony
Heavenly strains touch heartfelt emotions
Once forbidden in the silent zone
Sings louder, free will to aspire
To burst the silence travail
Echoes in the chamber's murky silence
Heaven cries out her sacred melody
Heart's love unyielding
In cantos of faith and hope
For the heart's forgiving purpose
Is to sing the songs of life
Living in joyous music
Filled with heavenly strains!

Jeffrey Elliott
San Jose, CA

Jeffrey E. Elliott has published two volumes of poetry with his daughter, Emily Jane Elliott: In Search of the Lost and In Search of the Lost, Volume Two: Look Toward the Light. These works have been successful and well-received by the public and critics alike; they are available on BarnesandNoble.com and Amazon. com. Jeffrey Elliott is an associate professor in the real estate department at Mission College in Santa Clara, CA. He also has a law practice in San Jose, CA.

Inspiration

Between school and homework,
Life and a full-time job,
Inspiration can be found.

After the paperwork
And the work,
No inspiration came to me.

And then I went to clean,
A brand new room to me;
A young lady in the hospital bed
Said to me,

"Poetry is what you make it,
Inspiration or no!"

Easter D. Morgan
St. Louis, MO

[Hometown] St. Charles, MO; [DOB] April 20; [Occ] housekeeper; [Hobbies] drawing, painting, dancing

Who Really Suffers, Me or You?

Why are you lonely, why are you sad, why are you weeping, why can't you be glad?
Why can't you be happy now that I am at peace, my new life's beginning with no pain or
disease? Are you weeping because I'm no longer with you? Why can't you realize I'm better off
than you? For you are the ones who really suffer and are living through the hassles that life has
to offer.

You have to see all the hatred and greed and people who fight to gain selfish need.
You have to live through the cheating and lying, that's why some of you, wish you too, were
dying. You have to live through all of the wars and see the pollution on God's ocean shores.
So why are you being selfish and wanting me there, to go through these hassles that you have to
bear?
You should be happy and thankful to God, for saving my soul and not letting it rot.

I am much better off than you, I'm praying someday you'll join me too.
For up here where I am there's no need to worry and to rush through life, there's no need to
hurry.
I can take each thing as it comes, for you see, my battle has been won.
I've been through the heartaches that life had to offer, now I'm much happier and don't have to
suffer.

Life is so peaceful and happy here and the things God offers are so very dear.
There are no such things as hatred or greed, only love that has grown from one small seed.
There is no sadness anywhere for God shows us He deeply cares.
He fills our hearts with His loving kindness, only His world is the absolute finest!

That's why I'm much better off than you and can't wait for you to join me too.
So please don't be lonely, weepy or sad, please don't be selfish … instead be glad.

Darlene Ware Horzepa
Ormond Beach, FL

A Letter to My Father

One day you were there and then you were gone
I waited for your return all along

A train in the distance I detected
Could take me to you? I felt rejected

Or the sound of an airplane in the sky
Would bring you back, so you could tell me why

Words about you no one ever spoke, as though
You were surrounded by a silent cloak
       Did you ever, ever think about me?

With time, I forgot the look of your face
Fantasies of you filled all of my space

I was a very little girl back then
Now, a grandma, I often wonder when

You've been in Heaven for many long years
Now when I think of you I shed dry tears

For the lonely years that we were apart
That unanswered question tucked in my heart
       Did you ever, ever think about me?

Ardyce Martin
Laguna Woods, CA

[Hometown] Chicago, IL; [DOB] December 19, 1936; [Ed] some college, insurance; [Occ] insurance agent; [Hobbies] writing poetry and short stories; [GA] mothering six children

My parents divorced when I was five years old, and I did not see my father again until I was sixteen; those years are what inspired my poem. Any child who grows up without a father carries sadness and pain that cannot be expressed—thankfully, poetry has allowed me to express mine.

Amongst the Reeds and Rushes

Amongst the reeds and the rushes, you ran,
With plimsoll, pinafore, precociousness—
I watched you amongst the weeds and the bushes.
Starched skirts enwrapped up, the flowers would match us;
We missed the noontime sun. The evening drew
Its hand over the day, the dusk would catch us.
In warmth, through my weighty eyes, I awoke.
Calm wine left in the basket had lulled me and
As I watched you play, I imagined how
Each blossom spoke, each stigma gave you words.
My conversation had passed, my tongue grew dry...
I forget their speech, the songs of the birds.
And as I watched your joy with each bound renewed,
I watched my voice grow old as it called out to you.

Emily Pylant
Austin, TX

[Hometown] Midland, TX; [DOB] February 10, 1994; [Ed] high school graduate; [Occ] unemployed poet; [Hobbies] reading, dancing, loving, singing; [GA] saving someone's life

The name's Emily, but I mostly go by Twink. I'm an odd person with many odd traits, and I love myself for it. It's thanks to my right-brained way of thinking that I'm able to explore many invisible worlds and create works such as this one. "Amongst the Reeds and Rushes" came to me quite out of the blue one day when I'd been reminiscing over an old friend and the times we'd shared. Yes, she was a beautiful girl with an old soul, and I loved her dearly. Please enjoy what she has inspired.

Romancing the Years

I can shrug away the wrinkles,
the graying hair, limbs less limber.
They are but the stamp of time!
Life sends me a love letter
for every day that passes.
What I still see,
what I remember,
I grasp with all my senses
and a grateful heart.
Life's romance is still mine
outlasting bonds of time.
A touch upon my shoulder,
A hand held tight in friendship
A song that echoes in my mind
Little children playing
Teens with awesome energy
All part of life's charm.
Swaying to a dance beat
Clapping hands at plays
I believe in romancing Life
In oh, so many ways.
Cynics would say, "It's over."
This, I don't believe
Every day's a new beginning,
So romance it, if you please!

Caryl Van Alstyne Shugars
Crossville, TN

[Hometown] Rochester, NY; [DOB] July 11, 1925; [Ed] BA from Denison University, thirty-one graduate hours from SUNY Brockport, NY; [Occ] teacher, store manager; [Hobbies] writing, painting, crafting, traveling [GA] raising three children to be respectful, productive, responsible and loving

What Might Have Been

Infants arrive not knowing what destiny awaits.
Carefree are the moneyed in their secure cliques,
as mankind carries burdens of emotional melange,
but despite cryogenics, all encounter eternal night.
Grave voices echo softly, "What might have been."

Babies become world citizens without consent,
they have no choice of country, race, or gender.
Infants arrive not knowing what destiny awaits.

Some struggle in offices and factories to prevail,
others find a niche to serve their supreme dream.
Carefree are the moneyed in their secure cliques.

Who has not tasted euphoric love, odious hate,
resentful envy, vicious evil or a narcissistic ego?
Mankind carries burdens of emotional melange.

Humans would take their prosperity with them,
but have not developed a functional conveyance,
and despite cryogenics, all encounter eternal night.

In maturity, all wonder about goals not achieved,
and time squandered without improving the psyche.
Grave voices echo softly, "What might have been."

Gordon Bangert
Vail, AZ

[Hometown] Weirton, WV; [DOB] June 26, 1930; [Ed] BS in business; [Occ] accountant; [Hobbies] games of skill; [GA] published prose and poems

In retrospect we have all realized late in life that we could have done something better, taken a risk or left a legacy to inspire others. This is my attempt to inspire a younger crowd to avoid saying what might have been.

Splendid Spirit

Man's splendid spirit
Embraces abundant joy
Revealing the soul

Human mystery
Death is but a beginning
Not the end of time

Treasures of the past
Precious seedlings to pass on
Remain forever

Memories illumine
Where we are in time and space
Glowing shining light

Man's splendid spirit
Embraces God's love and light
Golden canopy

Love and sorrow come
Engrossing our emotions
A star is gleaming

Man looks on the world
God looks on the human heart
Man looks on his goals

God looks on the soul
Draws us to eternity
Golden canopy

Loretta L. Morgan
Lacey, WA

[Hometown] San Francisco, CA; [DOB] November 6, 1926; [Ed] Seattle University, Seattle Pacific University; [Occ] retired Washington State ; [Hobbies] poetry, travel, gardening, birds; [GA] sharing life and love with family and friends

Haiku seeds contain thoughts gathered throughout my lifetime. These may be expressions of our Creator's love and light, or memories of the beautiful spirits who have entered my life at some point in time. All of this I have treasured and shared by writing haiku. These have become my prayer of thanksgiving for God's blessings.

Regrets

Looking through my memoirs
I see my life pass by,
Every page stirs a memory—
With some of them, I cry.
I cry for all the happiness,
I denied its pages;
These were all my doings,
Regrets are fool's wages.
Why could I not see then
As I see today?
How could I have been so foolish
And let love slip away?
He was all I ever wanted,
And he offered me a life.
How could I have hesitated?
I could have been his wife...
And now he's just a memory,
A love I let slip away.
Part of me went with him,
While part of me must stay.
And for now, I close the pages
On the remaining "wasted heap."
Yesteryear, I was foolish—
Today, I can sit and weep.

Hope Rodriguez
Kenner, LA

[Hometown] New Orleans, LA; [DOB] August 25, 1924; [Ed] two years of high school; [Occ] housekeeper, mother; [Hobbies] writing; [GA] the first poem of mine included in a published book

My name is Hope Rodriguez born 8/25/1924. I have been writing since I was a teenager. To me, it seemed an escape from boredom. As a quiet, young girl, I often would retreat to the privacy of my room, and there I would pour our all my pent-up opinions on issues. This was probably when I became fascinated with wording. Here, pen and paper were my only audience. And now it seemed I had found a "voice." While others talked, I chose to write. Maybe this was insecurity but it seemed very satisfying, and I continued to write about anything and everything. Through the years my biggest task seemed that of literally coming up with a word of rhyme that would still convey the true meaning of the sentence. This to me was like music, others called poetry.

Mother

I watched Mother through the window
Feeding the birds during the winter of color
Wearing Dad's green plaid work coat like many time
I noticed she'd grab his jacket and go
The cardinals with brilliant colors perched in a tree
While the gray doves gathered beneath her toes
The blue jays galloped in and around while
Mom struggled to stay on her feet in slippery snow
Nevertheless, the pail full of bird seed she did tote and go
Then smiled to herself after the job was complete
As she walked inside, wiping her hands and feet
Wearing a toboggan pulled down over her head
Then, I noticed the older image in the mirror
Was not Mother at all, but me instead

Anita Gardner
Drasco, AR

[Hometown] Heber Springs, AR; [DOB] August 20, 1943; [Ed] business and postal ; [Occ] administrative assistant for General Motors and postmaster relief; [Hobbies] gardening, flowers, writing; [GA] raising children and achieving a liberal arts college education

The Staircase

The staircase was, in ancient times, a way to reach divine
To greet the sky and wonder, to leave Earth in search of thunder.
Then the gods were harsher they punished every sin
So when you walked the stairway your life started to begin.
As the stairway made its way from ancient to refined
The steps that showed the way to life became a dream in human minds.
Slowly dreams became the myths, the legends told in rhymes
The gods were known in stories but all prayers to them were crimes.
So as legends whispered partial truths and wandered lost in time
Humanity roared bout its life and spread their unblessed rhymes.
Then the gods gave up their strength they turned from twelve to one
And legend says this one true God gave up his only Son.
But others held their own beliefs that God had blessed another
Great battles raged between the two
they forgot that they were brothers.
The staircase was, in ancient times a way to reach divine
But God looked down upon the earth and decided it was time.
Since man could not accept its fate and live as brothers should
The staircase was destroyed by God and faith was left for good.
The staircase once had given men the means to walk with gods
But men were bent on ruin, and their lives were wrought with fraud.
For loving one another as their God had told them to
Was replaced with hatred, mistrust became the rule.
The staircase is, in modern times, man's way to walk above
But golden rules are broken then hatred looks like love.

R. A. Lovelace
Tigard, OR

The Perfect Garden

The garden of old is a place without decay,
A world devoid of sonar harpoons or oil-ridden waters,
A place where no sign says
"Come back tomorrow."
The garden gate is open wide.
Why don't we go forward and step inside?
Instead, we hesitate and wait...as if
Nature had made a mistake.
Nature's plan needn't be abandoned or delayed,
As if creation was the cause of dismay.
We must listen to Earth's steady beat and not
Push aside seasons, as if they were cause for defeat.
No alterations are needed in this natural world sublime.
Earth's creation works in perfect time.
Who are we that we should stand without a plan,
Tearing everything apart upon this grand land?
Hasn't it been said and with praise,
"He saw what he had made and behold it was good?"
That statement must apply to lab mice too and all
Else that we view.

Gail Logan
Macon, GA

Some of my favorite poets are Robert Frost, T. S. Eliot, Emily Dickinson, John Keats, and Edmund Spenser; in fact, my MA thesis for the University of Rhode Island dealt with the classical influence in Spenser's "Mutability Cantos." I spent my childhood and adolescence in Wellfleet, MA, Cape Cod. My great loves are animals, nature, the sea and outdoors. I have accomplished a number of achievements in life, including learning a variety of skills and traveling widely. All of this has enabled me to live and enjoy a rewarding life.

Loveswept Love

Our love
is kept
it is windswept
After the rain
on the windowpane
you will keep
me
as we are in the
throws of our
loveswept love

Kathleen Ryan
Castro Valley, CA

[Hometown] *Castro Valley, CA* ; [DOB] *April 27, 1962;* [Ed] *BS in elementary education;* [Occ] *retired elementary school teacher;* [Hobbies] *romance books (reading and writing) and romance movies;* [GA] *receiving an award for my first published poem, "In Love's Breath"*

I like to read and write romance novels and poetry. I am from a family of six children and I keep myself busy by trying to keep up with my large family. I also like to do sewing and mending and have recently learned to do watercolor painting. I've had several poems published with Eber & Wein and want to publish a poetry book.

Thoughts from My Head

I sit at my desk and bang out poems
About things and events I have seen.
Inspirational thoughts, some not so much,
Some that should have never been.
But I'm compelled to write the words that I say,
And get them all off of my chest.
I hope they are read in the spirit they're written,
'Cause I'm trying to do my best.

I've lived many years and seen many things—
Some eventful, some happy, some sad.
I've known the love of a good woman,
I've experienced the death of my dad.
I have been there to see my children be born
And witness the lives that they lead.
I've shared with them in their abundance,
I helped them through their times of need.

I've seen a man walk on the moon
And the Rover take pictures on Mars.
In my next life I hope to experience the thrill
Of traveling out to the stars.
So in closing, I hope that you understand
That I'm sorry if my poetry reeks.
Remember, I'm doing the best that I can
In my search for the words that I seek.

Calvin Carter
River Oaks, TX

[Hometown] Fort Worth, TX; [DOB] May 22, 1952; [Ed] degree; [Occ] engineer; [Hobbies] karaoke [GA] yet to happen

This is a poem conceived at my computer. It began with the first line coming into my head and the rest just flowing out. It's a poem inspired by thoughts from my head and memories gleaned from my life. I hope you enjoy my poetry as much as I do writing it. Thanks for taking the time to read it.

Hidden

Every night tears slide down her face
and drop onto her pillowcase
Nobody can hear
because she cries silent tears
She cries herself to sleep
it is a secret that she will keep
Every day when she wakes
she puts on a smile that is fake
She tries her hardest to stay strong
so she acts like nothing is wrong
She doesn't want to seem weak
so strength she will seek

Ashley Weiland
Plymouth, MN

[Hometown] Crystal, MN; [DOB] October 10, 1996; [Ed] high school student; [Hobbies] writing and playing sports

Rose Petals and Antiseptic

Rose petals and antiseptic,
This is what's left of him.
This is where I leave a part of me
Forever.
I smell the rose petals,
But only see petunias.
I smell antiseptic,
But see no doctors.
I hear nothing,
But see the chatter.
I understand all,
But hope never to remember.
All dressed in black,
Not a sound is made.
Until from my weeping face,
A cry is displayed.
Rose petals and antiseptic
This is where his funeral was made.
Dressed in black,
This is where he stayed.

Yasmine Alamad
Schiller Park, IL

[Hometown] Schiller Park, IL; [DOB] August 9, 1997; [Ed] currently attending school; [Occ] hopefully, an author one day; [Hobbies] horse riding; [GA] publishing my first poem

Despite my young age, I have been through some very tragic occurrences. Most people dismiss my life-knowledge due to my age. This poem, along with others that have been published, are a few that have been written during these very tragic times. This particular poem was written when a very close friend of mine passed away abruptly. Writing helped me through his death, as well as through many other tragedies.

Inspired by Seuss

"Oh, the thinks you can think if only you try"
Dr. Seuss had it right
He made me believe in more
The beauty within the world
See one thing and twist it just right
Make it ugly and broken
Paint it colors of light
Then you shall see the new image
From another point of view
A new perception of the old
Turned new
Beauty comes in many forms
Just look at the core

Nicole Newton
Yorktown, VA

[Hometown] Tabb, VA; [DOB] August 3, 1983; [Ed] paralegal studies; [Occ] floral design; [Hobbies] writing; [GA] my book: Words from the Mind

I write in order to release what is pent up, and in doing this, I share my poems so people know they are not alone. I'm taking emotions and putting them into words.

Food Is Love

Food is a family tradition in one's home.
In a house, food is cooked from scratch creatively
Special days are even happier with cakes and sweets
With delicious homestyle recipes
A family will love simple customized meals
Serve the family the well cooked flavor they love
Make the brunch, add an "umph," as a secret weapon
Add a new twist to favorite recipes
Transform your Wednesday meals into something special
And let your creativity shine
A modern kitchen with good utensils give a vintage flare
Meals from the slow cooker offer comfort food without fuss
Birth in the word when it comes to budget friendly meals
Ground meat is great, thus use it to build a burger
Wine may be fine to drink
But for glaze it is glorious
Good recipes keep your ticker beating better
Stir the senses and say goodbye to stress
Cook your way through the garden of magic
Celebrate family time with your clan in your own way
And set the heart fluttering, for food bonds people
There stop your stomach rumbling
When you capture and sample the mouth watering dishes

Magiah Mageswari
Victorville, CA

[Hometown] Asia; [DOB] June 4, 1938; [Ed] enough to read and write; [Occ] housewife; [Hobbies] writing poetry, reading, cooking; [GA] cooking recipes coming out of magazines

Feet and Foot

Two feet and two foot(s) to use each day.
How many feet did your foot(s) carry you today?
We sincerely hope our precious feet don't lead us astray.
If such should happen, don't give up in dismay.
We look for the shortest route between here and there.
Many times upon arrival; we wonder why my feet
carried me here and there.
Make every foot count and appreciate with great joy.
Without two precious feet, we miss much to employ.
Be thankful for every foot your feet have carried you.
Give thanks to Heaven above for two precious feet,
Given to each with His love.

Hazel Eilers
Aberdeen, SD

[Hometown] Aberdeen, SD; [DOB] June 24, 1919; [Ed] teacher's certificate; [Occ] retired; [Hobbies] sewing, reading, cards, TV, writing; [GA] enjoying grands and great-grands

Ever since my childhood, I had hoped to become a teacher. I achieved my desire in 1939 after attending Northern State Teacher's College in Aberdeen, SD. I taught two years in Mansfield, SD. I broke my contract for the following year. Mr. Eilers appeared in my life. We were married for nearly sixty years and gifted with a family of nine children. My teaching days happily continued. My poem was inspired while getting a pedicure.

An Ode to Aging

Two years ago, I turned ninety.
When my synapses are snapped, I'm apt to be feisty.

I'm five feet-seven, give or take an inch,
My skin is all wrinkled, and my elbows itch.

My hair turned white, and my teeth turned yellow
But I'm hot to trot, and I feel quite mellow.

I haven't skipped rope in an awful long time
But in my mind's eye, I can do it just fine.

Life's biggest challenge is getting out of bed.
My joints say no, but yes is in my head.

In spite of my age, I have things I must do.
I need to shop for groceries and pay my taxes, too.

Next week, there's a birthday we will all celebrate.
Today I must order a very special cake.

So! All things considered, my life's still worth living.
I'll keep on taking, and I'll keep on giving.

I'll thank my God for my family and friends,
For my joys and sorrows, and whatever life sends.

Emily Fern Holswade
Alpine, NJ

[Hometown] North Hollywood, CA; [DOB] June 23, 1921; [Ed] high school and pierce school of nursing; [Occ] housewife; [Hobbies] reading, sewing, writing poetry; [GA] sixty-five years of marriage, four sons, six grandchildren

My twin sister and I were the youngest of eight siblings. Our growing years during the 1920s and '30s were spent in Southern California. Parental guidance taught us to appreciate what we had, to solve our own problems and honor our American heritage. During World War II, I worked for the Army Air Force, and my three brothers proudly served in the army and navy. Marriage in 1946 moved me to New York City where my husband completed his medical training, and I found work as a fashion model.

Desert Walkers

Propelled by an awakening need
for meaningful futures
      Javier, 19
      Ignacio, 21
cross the US/Mexico border
on foot at night
somewhere east of Nogales, Arizona.
The two young men trek northward
heedless of the dangers of a misstep
as death, stealth as a diamondback,
tags along their uncertain path
into the heat of the following day,
then strikes amid creosote and scorpion
leaving two vivid unfulfilled destinies
to drift forever upon desert sands,
as their mother kneels
before an image of the *Virgin of Guadalupe*
(painted by Javier at 15)
praying for the fulfillment
of her only sons' dreams

Ron Matros
Mesilla, NM

Zumwalt Prairie

Slow water seeps
From folds and cracks
Down to the pond,
Where, sated and slack,
It tries to deny
That it was the cause
Of the herring bone pattern
Of ridges and draws
That stitch the earth
From East to West
Like a bodice laced tight
Over Nature's breast.
 I can feel her breathing
Long and low,
Relieved to be free
Of the mantel of snow.
Her body is green
In a state of grace
As wildflowers bow
Where the zephyrs chase

Painted ladies
Circumscribed there
By the lazy shadows
Of the lords of the air.
 I float like a feather
In their mighty wings,
Drafting the currents
Of a perfect spring,
Counting the minutes
One by one,
Longing for when
My work will be done.
I'll lie on the hill
With the sun on my face
And welcome the return
Of my sense of place.

Gaynor Dawson
West Richland, WA

I have a cattle ranch on the Zumwalt Prairie where I spend my weekends working. During the week, I travel across the United States and internationally to consult on environmental matters. This poem reflects the comfort I take in returning to the land after hectic work schedules and endless hours on planes. It is one of many poems that will appear in my next book, Wallowa Song, echoing sentiments of poems in my first book, Yesterday's Moon.

Forever Friend

I know things of your past.
We shared so much, my friend.
As your mind begins to fade,
It's sad to see our sharing end.

Together we were children.
To school we walked each day.
Your talent as an artist …
 Beautiful creations always on display.

I feel the love you give …
And hugs shared with every visit.
Each time we talk together,
I ask God, "Just why is it?"

That everything is vague.
Nothing seems quite clear,
And yet your very heart
Seems to know whenever I am near.

I ask the Lord to bless you
Each day that you will live …
With caregivers filled with kindness
And every blessing God can give.

Patricia J. Mack
Livonia, MI

[Hometown] Livonia, MI; [DOB] April 13, 1941; [Ed] BA in education from Alma College, MA in education from Eastern Michigan University; [Occ] elementary teacher; [Hobbies] writing poetry, gardening and singing in my church choir; [GA] raising my own three children and affecting the learning and character for many students who, today, are contributing in vital ways to the diverse and challenging world in which we live

This poem was inspired by my childhood friend, Sandi. She has Alzheimer's and is in a care facility. I visit her, taking her for lunch, a movie, or sometimes a stroll in the woods. I am happy to see her smile and feel her hugs. She remembers me as "her best friend" and introduces me to her caregivers that way. We communicate on a different level now. The emotion I feel when her eyes light up is priceless. I know our special friendship is still there. I pray daily for Sandi's peaceful end to come only in God's gracious time.

My Family's Achievement Overshadowed My Own

My father is a retired policeman and C.A.D. counselor and my mother is a computer programer.

My family's achievement overshadowed my own
My family's achievement overshadowed my own

My sister is a nurse and she has been married two times and has four smart children.
They are all doing well, one is a school teacher, the other two are working on their careers.

My family's achievement overshadowed my own
My family's achievement overshadowed my own

My one half-brother shot himself in 2001 and in 2010 my sister's third son hung himself by accident. He was in college for art, he was only twenty years old.

My family's achievement overshadowed my own

But not today because I am sober today, so I can achieve whatever I want to today.

Dean Barcalow
Bordentown, NJ

[Hometown] Whiting, NJ; [DOB] September 24, 1958; [Ed] high school and college; [Occ] building service works; [Hobbies] biking and drawing; [GA] to be known by the writing world

I don't get my ideas from reading other books. They have been coming from what I have been going through in life. Since I stopped drinking and I haven't had ideas from TV shows or movies, I like reading about real people. This has not gone over big with my parents. They don't like the way I write because it is too realistic to them, and they don't think that any book I write will sell.

The Crooked Little House

I have a wonderful friend whom I truly love
Sent to me blessedly on the wings of a dove
It was time for her to move on with her life
So leaving behind memories and an old rusty knife
Taking only what she needed, and not much dough
She moved to a small town in central Colorado

She moved into a cute, crooked little house
I'm sure it was lived in by a sweet tiny mouse
It was on a crooked corner on a very busy street
Lots of weeds in the yard and dirt beneath her feet
It was in need of a lot of paint and repair
A little damage here, and some over there

Oh, but there was something about this place
It has charm and character, like an old lady's face
Around the front yard, a white picket fence
To her, it was perfect and made lots of sense
So she threw herself into fixing it all up
Friends and family helped, drinking from her cup

When it was done, oh my, was it looking good
All clean and fresh and strong where it stood
The house was still crooked and fairly little
Full of lots of love and a small brown fiddle
She's ready to start a new, challenging life now
Never forgetting the past, but moving on somehow

Now when I go visit her, and her son, in their crooked little house
We smile at each other, knowing there is no longer a sweet tiny mouse!

Beverly Rowland-Keenan
Lakewood, CO

I was inspired to write this about my incredible friend who was relentless fixing up her new home and how excited she was about it. I was so happy for her and her son and so very glad we are fast friends. The house is adorable.

The Human Race

What are the challenges that one must face
When being a runner in the human race?

There's so far to go, and so little time.
How do you start? Do you wait for a sign?

When the starting gun fires, and you're in the lead,
It's just human nature to go at top speed.

So, with all the challenges that one does face
Must we reach the point of a "basket case?"

Here is the answer, "slow down your pace"
Only Lord God will give you the grace.

Sandra Begeer
Santa Rosa, CA

[Hometown] Santa Rosa, CA; [DOB] June 1948; [Ed] Santa Rosa junior college; [Occ] clerical, customer service thirty years; [Hobbies] reading, writing, God-inspired poetry; [GA] being published by Eber & Wein

Infamous Enigma

Infamous enigma gone too soon,
wondering, mysterious soul walking on the moon.
Dazzling, talented, musical a famous enigma,
sadly a victim of mass media stigma.
Kind, generous loving pure inner child,
loud, electrifying, dancer so wild.
Black or white, black or white,
making the world's best music to Heaven's delight.
Infamous icon,
yet to three children normal loving father yet many fans at you cheered,
Yet misunderstood individual, dangled baby and many jeered.
Wonderful, deep, enigma, sweet, loving, mysterious,
his power caused many girls to faint with mass swept hysteria.
Eccentric, different, spontaneous, perfectionist,
humanitarian, generous, gentle, beautiful,
I believe is now on God's Heaven list.
Lived for 50 years, then you were gone,
but your life was a beautiful song.
Hope to see you in Heaven where life never ends
and hug me your loving fan and friend.
Just to add, I love you more.

Tina Jensen
Winchester, Hants, United Kingdom

Expressions

I'm looking at this paper
and don't know how to say,
That every time I see you
you take my breath away.
I sit and think to myself,
could this really be true?
I've prayed for the perfect man
and God brought me to you.
My love for you is too much to describe
but I know our love is so very strong.
You make all my dreams come true
and I promise to love you forever long.

Lacie Stoel
Naples, FL

[Hometown] Naples, FL; [DOB] April 10, 1986; [Ed] graphic design degree; [Occ] graphic designer and fashion designer; [Hobbies] video games, puzzles, gardening; [GA] college degree

God is to thank for my writing talent. As for inspiration, I have my fiancé to thank. He happens to be the subject of most of my work. I'm grateful to have the opportunity to share my feelings and express my emotions to others. God bless!

The Color of Pain

The head—frozen,
Red bloodshot eyes;
The slightest quiver
Sets off a heartbeat
That throbs throughout.
My body is sending shivers,
To the synapses
Of my brain screaming.
You idiot you know this
You're in the red,
All you see is red.
Angrily your brain sends
Shockwaves throughout,
Telling you, shouting
You're in pain...

Pamela K. Barger
Springfield, OH

[Hometown] Springfield, OH; [DOB] November 3, 1962; [Ed] computer programming; [Occ] author/ poet; [Hobbies] gardening, animals, reading, music, and movies; [GA] reading tutor and publishing my own poetry book

I've been writing poetry for most of my fifty years. It's always come easily and naturally for me. It is a hobby that has become a type of therapy—a cleansing of my soul, especially after I was diagnosed with systemic lupus. Like any chronic illness, systemic lupus is a difficult disease to navigate. Poetry helps keep me centered and in balance. I have been blessed with a talent, and I love sharing it.

What If

I gave in so I could gain, just like everyone else.
I want to get the feel of life for myself.
But what if I don't make it like most people do?
And what if I don't gain my joy like you?
Do I dig a little deeper to seek
or do I come up, and stop digging away peak after peak?
What if I reach out and touch life within?
What if I let it rule me, and teach me how to again and again?
What if I stop giving chase and just let things happen for a change?
Today, tonight, tomorrow, even if it does seem strange.
What if I follow up all of this with a cure?
And what if I get everything I want for sure?
But what if I don't achieve any of that?

Gloria McBride
Framingham, MA

*[Hometown] Beatrice, AL; [DOB] July 15, 1957; [Ed] twelve years, one year college; [Occ] disabled;
[Hobbies] singing, reading, writing poetry; [GA] getting printed, writing a book*

*Anybody's quest for love could lead anywhere—like on a desert island or on a flight in the air, even going for
a long drive trying to find you, when the feeling stops you and says, "This is it," this is you. Enjoy.*

Put Happiness First

I'm always movin' staying on top
My feet and body they never seem to stop.
I'm lean, I'm mean, my body is slim
I workout but I don't go to the gym.

In my head music tunes play inside
It keeps my body always stepping in stride
I'm small, I'm solid, my body so smooth
Creative, ambitious, come capture my moves.

I'm exciting to watch, my body flows free
I dress well, I look good, my clothes compliment me.
I owe my success to all of you for accepting my craziness, I express what I feel
You call me G. Q. Mr. Time, but what you see is what you get. I'm no phony, I'm the real deal.

My strong muscular body underneath
Inside my mouth, I still have my own teeth
The crowd watches me as I pass by
I keep on movin', give a wink of the eye

Don't need an iPod, cell phone, text 1-800 down load to go
Too much technology distraction makes you slow
Keep movin' to the music in your head
If you don't keep movin' you might as well be dead

Excuse me! These belong to you, your hearing aid, your scooter, your false teeth, your clapper,
    your cane,
All prescribed by your doctor, a footnote with your name.

John W. Johnson
West Berlin, NJ

[Hometown] Paulsboro, NJ; [DOB] March 23, 1944; [Ed] high school (tech, music, military); [Occ] tech, post office (retired); [Hobbies] art, music, cook, travel, sing, and dance; [GA] saving lives

I'm retired now, I write, sing, dance, draw, cook, landscape, decorate and traveled all my life. People always compliment me on my appearance and my approach to life in general, my generosity and honesty to myself and others. I joke around about everything; it doesn't hurt to make someone smile. My writings are for enjoyment to educate and inform one's mind, like a lost soul looking for direction to find. I have some poetry on my Facebook page.

"G" for "Godly"

Why "G" for "Godly?" I heard a student ask.
Father God is in Heaven; He can't tell when we're off task.
What's the point of going green? Jesus Christ is seldom seen.
Giving us blue for talking too much is really being mean!
Why "G" for "Godly" when I'm such a mellow fellow?
Who cares if I'm not paying attention? I should never draw a yellow!
So I'm not prepared for class; throw that orange in the trash.
Give me a break, I can barely stay awake!
And about that purple for being unkind,
my buddies don't care when I speak my mind!
Why go for Godly when my past behavior landed me on red?
All my parents really did was send me to bed.
Why go for "Godly" behavior? So what if I land on red?
All my parents ever do is send me to bed.
Why should I behave in school?
No one follows the "Golden" rules.
Even the House of Congress fusses and fights;
Nobody cares anymore about being right.

Ruby Waller
Las Vegas, NV

[Hometown] Las Vegas, NV; [DOB] March 14, 1955; [Ed] bachelor degree; [Occ] education; [Hobbies] writing; [GA] raising my children then finishing my education

As the thirty-fifth birthday of my firstborn, Ebony Waller, approaches on October 18, 2013, I am reflecting back on the amazing life God has provided and nurtured for me. It started with Him being the amazing father that breathed life into me and passed down His knowledge of spiritual things. Then He entrusted me with a wonderful mother named Willie Mae Stewart who gave birth to me and nurtured me through the trials and tribulations of life. Then He gave me the strength to endure a father who made me the strongest daughter on Earth teaching me how to heal my pain and grow with the Grace of God. Then he sent me a husband to father my children and help me to raise them to the beautiful people they are today. Then when Satan thought he had me and my family buried deep in sadness and poverty, and sin and shame, God sent a man named Barack H. Obama to reform the land and restore our hope for a bright future for our children. Today, faith and hope are still working out for our family. I followed my Christian School as poetic justice for the school's disciplinary action plan.

reach for your dreams

dream, some say big
we are taught not to give up on them
do not be afraid
dare
see yourself living it
being it
doing it
wildest
life is fluid
like a dream
doesn't always make sense
it is in the effort that we thrive
not in the having landed at some station along the road
let yourself dream
big
wild
believe
nothing is out of reach

Lisa Schwab
Playa Del Rey, CA

[Hometown] West Los Angeles, CA; [DOB] January 5, 1962; [Ed] Santa Monica College; [Occ] restaurant owner; [Hobbies] reading, writing, watching movies; [GA] living my dream

I own and operate an Italian restaurant in Playa Del Rey, CA. I was raised by my Italian grandparents and I am honored to keep their memory alive. My grandmother's cooking, my grandfather's music, taught me about love, family and tradition. I credit my childhood for my imagination; I was the only child in our home, which turned out to be a great opportunity to dream.

Of Silk and Dust

The cocoon falls loose from the branch
Softly wafting to the ground
Gently landing on top of a coverlet of fall leaves

The hiker exploring
Enjoying the brightness of the autumn day
Fresh cool air, caressing his senses

The boot comes down upon the leaves
Smashing the silky cocoon
Now dust in the air

The butterfly is gone, so delicate and fragile
Never to decorate the landscape with its lovely beauty
Or infuse hope into our hearts with its flitting dance

The trees drop some more autumn leaves
Crying at the loss of their beautiful friend
But knowing more will rise again

Like the butterfly made of silk and dust
Life will wrench the most from us
But the dreams we store up in our heart
Life can't take, can't take apart

Marcy L. Bowser
Newark, OH

[DOB] September; [Ed] two years college; [Occ] supply technician; [Hobbies] poetry, camping with my husband; [GA] raising my children

I love writing poetry; I compare it to making music with words. This poem is basically talking about the beauty of life and the fragility of the heart and soul—how hard it is to hold onto our dreams, and how we shouldn't give up on our dreams. I am a Christian; thinking about how much Jesus loves us is always an inspiration to me.

Reagan's War

On 1945, the end of World War II.
Just two superpowers would be:
Union of Soviet Socialist Republic, think new,
United States of America to relieve.

Germany's defeat soon became divided,
East and West Germany being the site.
A wall built in Berlin gets divided,
Both are given a special control cite.

Soviet ships and submarines cover the world.
 Eastern Europe, Soviets would depreciate.
Radio, Reagan worked—showed power to the world—
Radio free Europe, made people motivate.

Soviets move into a few countries,
Become helpful in some ways.
Underground unit in Eastern Europe countries:
SDI gets help from USA in those days.

Soviets lost the war in Afghanistan,
Unable to help their allies.
USA helps free countries with Reagan,
The 40th President to improve their lives.

Arvid Homuth
St. Charles, IL

[Hometown] Valley City, ND; [DOB] February 13, 1929; [Ed] Jamestown High School, VC State (BA), NDU (science, printing); [Occ] printing industry, linotype operator for twenty-five years; [Hobbies] oil painting, playing piano [GA] being featured in the University of Illinois Art Show

I found an interesting book to read about Ronald Reagan. He is perhaps the least understood president of the twentieth century. His life seems a conundrum, his ways a mystery. Reagan's War, by Peter Schweitzer (copyright 2002) inspired me to write this poem. The Communist party had been active in Hollywood since 1935 with headquarters in New York City calling for the capture of Hollywood's labor unions. Reagan was a member of this Hollywood labor union. Reagan had his first conflict with communism and began confusing the Russians and the Americans.

The Vibrance of the Stones

All the stones have eyes
Her eyes were iron stones
The pebbles hear her sunset sighs
As they're burying her bones
They watch her last breaths rise
Evaporated, wretched moans
The music of her disguise

Now the pebbles, with tired eyes
From their life in war-torn zones
Refuse to utter even the smallest lies
Because they are not her drones
And as they begin to realize
That they're human, not her clones
They finally shatter their granite guise

And freed, emancipated from that life-long vise
The pebbles cease their groans
And celebrate her hard demise
For now she for never, ever owns
The substance of their lives

Her eyes were iron stones

All the stones have eyes

Rev. Rebecca Guiles Hudson, MA
Belen, NM

[Hometown] Belen, NM; [DOB] January 31, 1953; [Ed] MA in counseling; [Occ] certified peer counselor for the mentally ill, poet, minister, counselor; [Hobbies] writing, singing, serving others; [GA] through the grace of God many people chose not to commit suicide because of my help

We live in a society that teaches us to always put family first, regardless of what kind of maniacs and ogres constitute that family. We are taught through guilt and obligation that it's not okay to put ourselves and our own needs first, and it's almost impossible to shed that cultural blanket of toxic bonds. This poem is an anthem to it being all right to celebrate, not grieve, a monster's passing—even when that monster was closely related to us. And it's okay to live a guilt-free, unburdened, honest life, manifesting and expressing our deepest, most personal truths without regret.

John's Choo Choo

It started as a hobby
A train track he was to make
With all kinds of track
and buildings and maybe a lake.

He placed the platform on a board
With tracks going right and left
With trains, all kinds, cabooses and all
Engines and coal cars too big to heft.

He hooked them up to the electric
With switches here and there
Then there was a tunnel
In a mountain over here.

He worked to make it interesting
With hills and trees galore
He added as time went by
A passenger train and more.

Eventually, there will be houses
With people here, cars and streets to see
A village with stores all around
And whatever more can be.

When it's finished with benches
A park, street lights so we can see
Then the trains go racing by
What a hobby it turned out to be.

Jeannie Urban
Fairfield, IA

I have written poetry since I was fifteen, and now I'm eighty-three. I love it. I have won several awards, and my poetry has been published in twenty books. I've won a huge award, along with several small ones. I had lots of fun doing this. Thank you.

Ole Bud

"Ole Bud" is my brother
   he chews, he spits
He's wiry, he's windy,
   he chomps at the bit

He's articulate, he's gifted
   he has talent galore
He's lived with a passion
   for life ever more

And now Ole Bud has
   time none to spare
Old age has crept up
   but Ole Bud doesn't care

He sleeps when he's tired
   and eats when he's ready
He meets each new day
   with hands none too steady

His steps may have slowed
   his eyes have grown dim
But tomorrow is beckoning
   Ole Bud's off on a whim

Jean Brendlinger
Aurora, MO

[Hometown] Aurora, MO; [DOB] October 14, 1925; [Ed] high school; [Hobbies] *writing, puzzles, singing;* [GA] *my poem published*

I'm eighty-seven and have problems—my hands make it hard to write. I've been writing since I was fifteen years old but never dreamed of being published until now.

Circle of Love and Winds

Women standing alone with themes of love—
appearances of children, in the placement of trails and slopes of snow.
Thoughts of you made me remember the last time
we knew each other's happiness, all that love...
And still, there is loneliness that comes back with this intelligence.
You know I still love you, as I always will; and I know,
somehow, you still love me.
Somehow, somewhere, appearances happen with memories of love.
May you always know that part is still there for you, my dear husband.
Every day, our abstract notion thinks we have to learn
as we glide through nature, together, alone—whatever—it is,
still is, the same as it was. No one can ever change that.
Our energy is not destroyed.
Will you at once know who is there with you, please?
Or shall I guess that our love was complete, as always?
The many we know can be with you in prayer,
as God would have us remember Him.
Now this Easter, passion of Lent, reminds me
not to have anything without respect for our Lord as Savior.
You stand out there, without me.
How can you like it, when I love you
with all my heart and soul, from before?
Don't you know she cannot be me, only, but you as me?
When we married, we were with God, and now
they can cherish her forever—like a wife,
a girl, and a woman with her family.

Meggan Thomsen
Tappan, NY

*[Hometown] Tappan, NY; [DOB] August 14, 1951; [Ed] VCU, Harvard University, Parsons New School;
[Occ] artist, designer, teacher; [Hobbies] swimming, skiing; [GA] retrospective*

*"Circle of Love and Winds" is inspired by change. As time goes by, our families, as well as ourselves, seem to
undergo a kind of makeover from what and who we were before. As a response to this, our loving relationships
and personalities need to adjust to the new day with the traditional structure—as it was, or as it still is.
"Circle of Love and Winds" gives thought to family and friends. May you always enjoy reading this piece.
Thank you.*

A Drop of Water

I am a lonely drop of water
cast away from my home, the sea
for reasons unknown to me
Someday, the sun
with its brilliant rays
will warm me up
to the state of non-existence
To the naked eye, it seems
but by the process
of evaporation and liquefaction
I will return to my home, the sea
God is the sea
we are just drops of water

Mercedes Moncion
Arlington Heights, IL

[Hometown] Arlington Heights, IL; [DOB] August 18, 1935; [Ed] MD, post-graduate training; [Occ] retired; [Hobbies] painting; [GA] raising five children

I am a retired physician who practiced family medicine for about thirty years. I have written several poems; some of them have been published, and I hope someday to publish a book. I was born in the Dominican Republic and have been living here in the US for the last fifty years.

Good Friends

Good friends listen to each other
Don't try to hurt or smother
Good friends don't try to put each other down
Don't like to see each other drown
Good friends try to understand
Don't try to be in command
Good friends read each other's moods and feelings
Can even pull you off the ceilings
Good friends help each other solve a problem
They're willing just to talk and solve 'em
Good friends give each other compliments
Sometimes, we could use the pick-me-up a bit
Good friends can disagree without hurting each other
It's okay, you love them like no brother
Good friends you can trust
Good friends are a must
Good friends give each other room for change
Even give room to range
Good friends care about each other
You love them like there is no mother

Kathy A. Mathews
Claremore, OK

[Hometown] Claremore, OK; [DOB] December 25, 1950; [Ed] high school, some college; [Occ] retired bookkeeper, homemaker; [Hobbies] sewing, reading; [GA] being published and continuing to write poetry

Raised in Claremore, OK—home of the legendary Will Rogers—I grew up loving God and country, along with family and friends who fill my world with all the love needed to keep me busy writing my poetry that is cherished forever by my grandchildren.

To Tell the Truth?

What's up with so many untruths?
The headlines scream, "Scandals"
Newspapers and news TV salivate for more Lions roaring for food
Talking heads to
Parrot and repeat statements
Given from higher-ups
Some say white lies are necessary
To achieve hidden agendas
Keeping people unaware in the dark
Don't rock the already shaky boat
Snooping by the IRS
False reports about Benghazi
Jury trials and racism
Stock market numbers made to entice
The press reports? We decide?
Not enough information that is reliable

Sandra Glassman
Oceanside, NY

[Hometown] Oceanside, NY; [Hobbies] writing, teaching, music; [GA] musical composition in Holocaust museum

I am a published poet and songwriter. My music can be heard on WNBR.FM in Nashville, TN. I have written over two thousand poems, and my poetry reflects all topics—from nature to politics to love and romance, and anything that sparks creativity! I have videos on YouTube.

Old Feet

My old feet walked many a mile.
Long ago I walked down the aisle.

I have nothing to hide,
From traveling far and wide.

I have seen the sunset from the hills,
As I sat by the table writing out the bills.

I have been from sea to sea.
There is no greater place to be.

I have traveled many a street,
Using these old worn out feet.

I was often red as a beet,
From walking in the heat.

I can say I have walked every season,
Though I do not know the reason.

I have taken a lot of teasin'
But it was downright pleasin'

Tell every Tom, Dick, and Harry, and don't forget Pete,
You should always take care of your stinky old feet.

Evelyn Rose Schmidt
Williamsburg, IA

[Hometown] Williamsburg, IA; [DOB] February 6, 1941; [Ed] valedictorian; [Occ] writer (poems/songs); [Hobbies] music, poems, country and blue grass songs; [GA] featured artist of USA and the world in poetry

My friends, I have written and published many poems and songs throughout the USA and Europe. I was often chosen as the featured artist of the USA and the world in many anthologies. I love writing the words to country and folk songs. Many of these songs and poems have a story to tell and a lesson to learn from the days of long ago. One must always speak from the heart. The truth is, one does not always take good care of his feet. When one can no longer walk, then you realize how important it is to care for your feet. Oh, clock on the wall, do tell...won't you please turn back the hands of time to yesterday when I lived the old-fashioned way? When I was young, I stood youthful and tall. Now I look in the mirror and I look so small. One must enjoy life and perhaps see some of the places in the world while one is able to travel using your tired "Old Feet."

My Super Hero

We so often hear the words;
      My hero
What makes a hero in our eyes?
Is it the one who wiped away a tear,
The person who caught wild
Kitty cats for 2 children?
Is your hero the person who
Taught you how to fix many a thing?
Or is a hero the mailman, fireman, policeman,
The brave soldier who is away from family,
Friends, and everyday life?
Heroes come in many shapes and sizes, but
the hero in my life is my daddy.
He was the person I could talk to about anything,
The person who disciplined me with unconditional love.
Daddy, you are in Heaven now but you are still my hero.
And, Daddy, you are with my superhero, Jesus.
Thanks for being my hero.

Lydia C. Wilson
Killen, AL

This poem, prose, ode or verse was sent to my mind by the one and only superhero in my mind, and that is Jesus Christ, my personal Lord and Savior.

Mirror Mirror

I look in the mirror and say good morning and it looks back at me and says *hi you're ugly and I hate what I see, no amount of makeup can help you.* But, I learned mirrors are mean and even though you don't think you're beautiful someone out there does and I'm glad I found the one who thinks I am. And though the names might follow me in the halls and the things that people might say, this person will in time make all those bad memories go away and help my scars to heal. Like they said, time will heal all wounds. And I know that this person will always love me for who I am. I am Kailey Skye Francis Korner.

Kailey Korner
Macungie, PA

[DOB] April 26, 1998; [Ed] in high school; [Hobbies] art, singing; [GA] being published and being a big sister

Understanding Love

"Did I really know love until I trusted you,
And trusted myself at the same time?
Sheltered throughout life, how was I to recognize love?
Never fully explained, not fully understood."

I hid what I felt because I couldn't explain
Or deal with what was going on inside.
I was once told that love was you
Wanting to make the other person happy.
No matter whether you were or not.

But this is way beyond that.
Yes, I want him happy; but even more
I want him to have all his dreams
And will do everything within my power to do so,
Even calling on bridges thought previously burned.

Once I allowed myself to think of him like that,
To get over being so scared,
I fell hard, deep, and extremely fast.
I used to not be able to explain
Or have any real understanding of love.

I understand now.

Pamela Michelle Perry
Oklahoma City, OK

I have been writing poetry for over twenty-five years. My family and friends say if you ever want to know how I feel, just read my poems. This is about my boyfriend, whom I have known since we were children. I never knew what my grandmother meant until I stopped hiding and allowed myself to feel.

Song of a Wild Dove

Coo coo coo…
Perching on the backyard apple tree
Singing a swingy pattern
Creating a doleful concern
A soft music for the beloveds oversea

Coo coo coo…
We grew up in the same settlement
Birdsong recalls old days
Oh breeze brings my heart away
Through the clouds to previous events

Coo coo coo…
Awful situation separated our lives
Away from green forests
Rivers and mountain crests
The harmony of insects in the wild

Coo coo coo…
Soon the sky will miss the sunray
Passion inspires the dove
Fulfilling my heart with love
Of all the dearest dispersed far away

Xaysouvanh Phengphong
West Valley City, UT

[Hometown] West Valley City, UT; [DOB] October 17, 1950; [Ed] Salt Lake Community College; [Occ] Operator; [Hobbies] writing poems and short stories

Phengphong is a well-known poet/writer in Laos and Esan, a citizen of Thailand since 1996. He is a French high school graduate as "Bachelier en Mathematiques et Sciences de la Nature." He was an AF Pilot in the Vietnam War and an airlines captain for sixteen years. At fifteen, he began his poetry. Lao and French classic literature was a solid foundation of his artistry. His poems are published in America at the Millennium, Great Poems of the Western World, Great Poets Across America, International Who's Who in Poetry, Today's Best Poets *and others. He is a resident of West Valley City, UT, founder/advisor of "Lao Poetry Society," a worldwide organization. His Unique Moon compilation was published in 2012. Read in Lao, Thai, and English at xppppw.blogspot.com.*

Inequality

Until science and technology advances to where
parents can choose which chromosomes their offspring gets,
What can we do besides abstinence or accept it?
If everyone was the same, we wouldn't be individuals;
If nobody had flaws, how would doctors and surgeons stay employed?
Is it our hues that make us who we are—
Our varieties of complexions, shapes, heights, widths,
Sexual orientations or levels of intelligence?
Despite these, we're still each a person at the end of the day,
Although some of us are belittled, stereotyped, racially profiled, biased,
Disowned and sometimes excommunicated for being different.
We still inhale oxygen, have feelings and exhale carbon dioxide,
Including others that require a medical ventilator.
The discrimination and maltreatment leaves victims vulnerable.
To defend ourselves, we have to deflect the insults
And stand firm and strong as an activist or civil rights leader
How can someone hate all of one race or type without
Knowing each person of it individually?
The snobby and conceited prosper, while people in poverty suffer.
This is backwards, like a parent who would bring a child to the store
And the child cries for a one-dollar candy bar
The parent rejects it, but spends eight dollars for cigarettes.
They won't spend one dollar to satisfy the child,
But will spend eight dollars to kill both of them

Kendrick O. Williams
Fort Worth, TX

[Hometown] Birmingham, AL; [DOB] August 27, 1984; [Ed] Stratford Career Institute; [Occ] retail manager; [Hobbies] http://poetmindpollution1.com; [GA] being awarded the title of International poet of merit

I am a multiple award-winning poet/writer. Mindpollution is my business website. www.poetmindpollution1. com. This poem was written in honor of Trayvon Martin, Al Sharpton and Jesse Jackson, as well as anyone who has experienced racism or discrimination, including homophobia. As the Constitution states in the preamble, "All men are created equal, that they are endowed...with certain unalienable rights, that among these are Life, Liberty, and the Pursuit of Happiness." Life is taken by murders, pursuit of happiness is taken by discrimination and preventing same-sex marriages; liberty is also removed by murders and imprisonment.

My Mother

She was born May 2, 1924
you might think what do I care for?
Now I believe that I will never see that friend
to maybe when my life will come to an end
But I'm going to hope and pray
that we can meet again someday
She was so very unique and wonderful
her heart and soul was so very beautiful
White, yellow, red, yes people who were even black
friends are one thing she didn't lack
She treated everybody so fair
rich or poor, she didn't care
There wasn't anybody she didn't treat kind
no matter how many friends she would find
She never had a bad name for anyone
no matter what they've done
She was the best friend I ever had
even better, much better, than my dad
One thing she did that wasn't that good
she let people walk over her whenever they could
She was like an ace
my love for her can't be replaced
I guess this is too long
but I can't say so long
Well, this is the end
to my never-forgotten friend
By now you know there is no other
than the love I have for my mother

Allan Richard Minkowsky
Saint Petersburg, FL

[Hometown] Saint Petersburg, FL; [DOB] May 11, 1949; [Ed] high school; [Occ] retired; [Hobbies] writing poetry; [GA] getting three anthologies from poetry.com

My poetry relaxes me. I feel good after writing my poems.

The Magic of Love

It starts out as a thought of affection,
hopefully with no rejection.
A feeling of warmth, love and charm,
combined with a strong embrace in your lover's arms.
A joy of excitement nurtured not in haste.
A steady pace of installments of pleasure
and each dose carefully measured
as if it was a golden treasure.
Like a totally complete surprise,
right before my very eyes
an event that is never tragic,
yet it seems just like magic.
When a child is first brought into this world
from the mother's womb,
a new heir springs out
and gives out a mighty shout.
This is the magic of love.
Just like a dove sent from above,
life has entered the world again.
With love, this process will never end!

Brian Cook
North Hollywood, CA

I felt a compassion to express my happiness about my newborn niece Vivian Cook. This was the motivating factor for conjuring up this particular poem. The birth of a child is like magic from God Himself.

Timely Thinker

My mom is a brilliant eighty-six
Her life experience has taught her lots of tricks!
She can remove a stain quick as a wink
She can tighten a spare tire faster than I can think!
She can cut and sew a pattern from paper in a bag
She can whip up a meal from leftovers without a brag!
But she has a problem that, at times, just hurts my head
Her computer is so slow that a turtle would win instead
I mean, really...
It clicks and clacks and thinks so very hard
One would truly believe
That its brain would be totally charred
I have a difficult time waiting for it to think
I always end up pushing buttons—
That leaves many chores in the brink!
The sweet, old thing does finally get to the point
But by the time it does
I'm ready to go screaming from the joint!
I wish I could talk her into a newer tower
She would really appreciate the speed
And mind-blowing power!
But...she likes what she has, she says it understands
And she doesn't mind the wait
She hopes that I am patient with her...when she is ninety-eight

Linda S. Wicker
Lansing, MI

[Hometown] Lansing, MI; [DOB] December 2, 1948; [Ed] high school, AT&T, Lucent Technologies; [Occ] project manager, system programmer; [Hobbies] crafting, writing; [GA] my daughters

My poem "Timely Thinker" is inspired by my mother who is eighty-six and she refuses to say she is old yet. She has had her computer since my brother went to serve in Iraq. He gave her the computer so they could keep in touch by e-mail. I taught her how to use it, and the poem says the rest.

Yours from the Start

Take what's left of your pride,
swallow the pain.
The tears are falling
just like rain.

I didn't even see you
walk away.
You were suddenly gone
just like yesterday.

I never should have let you
read my poem.
I should have left my feelings
for you unknown.

Don't worry
you didn't break my heart.
You just took it with you;
it was yours from the start.

Cyndi S. Carlsgaard
Rockwell, IA

[Hometown] Albert Lea, MN; [DOB] March 7, 1965; [Ed] AAS retail management; [Hobbies] writing poetry, going on nature walks; [GA] marrying the love of my life

The House with No Doors

I found a house that had no doors.
I went in as though it was calling me.
And as I entered the house, I could hear the wind as it drifted in
Through the windowpane.
Then I heard something. The walls, the walls were speaking
they were whispering,
"I have secrets to share, so many to tell."
And so then I sat and listened to secret after secret,
Each sounding more familiar than the previous.
And as I heard the final secret the walls wished to share,
It was then that I realized, these were my secrets.
My deepest thoughts and darkest fears.
Had the walls really talked?
Or was it just my confessions to the wind?

Tori A. Hernandez
Bakersfield, CA

I have always had a love for writing, but I never really pursued it until the death of someone close to me. Writing gave me an outlet to express the feelings I just couldn't get out. Now without encouragement from my family and the never-ending support and encouragement from my junior high English teacher, I don't think I would still be writing. I am blessed.

Cherish

I would guide my soul to you
bound to feel like a seagull
and between enchantment and charm feel
peace you give to me
I would be the dawn of a warm sunrise
Finding you feeling my love everywhere
and in your arms and insatiable
Be a woman, mad with passion
Being one, love, just one
be the total charm
that every night we wrap
with the single breath
partner and progress being
I would walk up to you and feel
we are a casual love
Fruit of a day without a par
that gave us the desire to wander
I would feel that whisper heat
of that delicious pun
radiating and radiating joy
after a late response
Being one, love, just one
be the total charm
that every night we wrap
with the single breath
partner and progress being

Lorena M. Soto
Reynoldsburg, OH

[Hometown] Reynoldsburg, OH; [DOB] August 21, 1961; [Ed] degree in business administration, marketing, advertising, and public offices; [Occ] CEO VHPPC Tax Services Provider, multi-lingual interpreter, marketing consultant; [Hobbies] travel and writing poetry in six different languages

I dedicate this poem to all beings in love with life and love; I dedicate these lines with love and tenderness to each and every one of you to have in mind that love is the purest and most genuine feeling; it must be looked after, loved, and respected. Love is the food we should not miss in our lives to make it more rich and positive. Let us always be open and honest with ourselves to live fully love. I am Lorena Soto and I dedicate these lines with all the love that I have for the state of Ohio, my home, my sweet home. I thank my parents for who I am from the bottom of my heart. Thanks, Mom and Dad.

Nighttime Prayer for Jaime

As I close my eyes
I pray the Lord for a restful sleep
With a choir of angles singing in my dreams
And waking me up filled with His love and peace.

Elizabeth A. Garcia
Edinburg, TX

I was blessed as big sister of an extra special angel. My younger brother, Jaime, was born with special needs. A few years ago, before he passed away, he slipped into coma for several days. When he was released from the hospital I was inspired to write Jamie his own prayer. As I said the prayer each night with him, it was my "Thank You" to God blessing my life.

Near to a Promise

A day that is mild
perfect as a dream
with its evening wrapped in colors
of mauve, peach, silvery-lavender and cream...
a bouquet chosen for me
made from rose petals
with a fragrance everlasting
sunshine, gentle winds
and birds' songs to command my morning
A place sealed with beautiful thoughts
a quiet time to pray
Very near to a promise
of our tears being wiped away
within my soul, an embrace
a time and place serene
I must reach for my Jesus' hand
to lead me.

Helen Roark
Coal City, WV

[Hometown] Pipestem, WV; [DOB] February 28, 1947; [Ed] high school graduate; [Occ] homemaker; [Hobbies] writing poetry

I usually write spiritual poems and, since 1993, some have been published. I enjoy writing about God's love and promises. We all go through times of illness, sadness and loved ones passing away. We all can find it comforting when we write about God's faithfulness!

Beatitude

She's kneeling there at the altar,
Wrapped in time,
Nearing Eternity,
Her head bowed
In white-haloed proof
Of life's unrelenting burdens.
Beads slip through hands
Mangled by daily toil...
Earth's outcast.
Waiting for release.

I sit chastened,
Humbled by my life of ease.
Few cares mar my lotioned hands.
As I remember the widow's mite,
With envy I hear His words:
"Blessed are the meek.
Blessed are the poor."

Christine Ruland
Macungie, PA

This aging process brings on new perspectives. We notice different things and they take on meaning that we haven't thought about in youth. In my former life I have taught and been a secretary, also raised six children. My husband is now suffering with Alzheimer's which puts everything into new realms of experience. Thus the sight of a woman in church inspired this poem.

Untitled

Begot my soul upon an Earthen bed
Through the struggle and the strife
Mother's gentle hands did rest upon my head
That she should teach me all the ways of life
The words of women and the trials of men
Deboule between them like a fighter
Although they crossed too desperately and when
they do she ended with an "angel py-er"
Wherefore your eyes do look to God?
The soul brought forth is reaching its full bloom
My mother's words of him shook and awed
His face were all the lights inside the room
Though your body be weak and tired, Ile Waste
Your spirit will always be my Sukawaka Cante

Rachel Kristeen Morgan
Richmond, VA

I wrote this sonnet for my mother, Catherin Ann Morgan, for her last Mother's Day. My mother lived an incredibly full life, and I wanted to try to capture as much of it as I could. She was my teacher, friend, confidant, and mother. I will always love and remember my Momma Morgan.

Remember Lot's Wife

For those who are severely tempted to do wrong

In the Old Testament, Lot was the nephew
of Abraham who lived in the city of Sodom located
on the plain of Jordan near the Dead Sea. Sodom was
destroyed by a fire from Heaven because of the
wickedness of the inhabitants. The Holy Bible warns us
to "Remember Lot's Wife." She had escaped the doomed
city filled with wickedness and strife. Abraham questioned
God "Would the righteous be destroyed with the
wicked?" Abraham asked God to spare the city of Sodom
if various numbers of righteous residents could be found.
Ten righteous residents were not found; thus Sodom was burned
into the ground. Fleeing the coming destruction, Lot's
Wife left most of her possessions, family and friends behind. Sodom
had been her life, and I imagine she was crying. The rescuing
angel warned Lot and his wife not to look back, but to keep making tracks.
Lot's wife looked back more than she ought, and suddenly turned into
a pillar of salt. Her story is a warning for us today.
We need to keep our soul-destroying sins at bay. When
you have escaped from corruption in the world, do not go
back to give it one last swirl. There may be seven more
demons to fight. You may never escape again from your plight,
although your vice may appear harmless and light. "There is
a way which seemth right unto a man, but the end thereof are the ways of death." Proverbs
chapter 14, verse 12. Both body and soul of the wicked will be destroyed in hell fire. (See
Matthew chapter 10, verse 28)

Bernice Hooks
Los Angeles, CA

[Hometown] Los Angeles, CA; [Ed] Graduate LACC, mission renaissance art school; [Occ] entrepreneur,
Cambridge Who's Who; [Hobbies] drawing, painting, swimming, singing hymns, sewing; [GA] author of
Reflections Before Dawn Volume 1

Love

Love shouldn't be a battlefield
holding out swords and holding up shields.

Love should be forgiving.
Love shouldn't be forfeiting.

Love shouldn't be arguments
Where we both start throwing fits.
Love should be both of us giving
in just a little bit.

Love's supposed to have laughter
and can truly be happy ever after.

Joan Williams Krueger
Bastrop, TX

[Hometown] Bastrop, TX; [DOB] April 23, 1984; [Occ] CEO Forever Love Antiques; [Hobbies] singing, writing, playing with my children; [GA] life in general

My inspiration for this poem came from feelings about my husband and our relationship.

Memorial Day

My daughter looked at me across the dinner table.
"Did you pray for the dead today?"
I frowned at her and swallowed my mashed potatoes.
"It's Memorial Day. Did you pray for the dead today?"

"It's the day we remember those
who died for our country." I said.

"Well, did you remember them?
Did you pray? I did." And then she fled the table.

My conscience pinched.
I hadn't remembered my immigrant uncle,
dead before I was born, buried in Flanders Field.
Gathering the dishes, I remembered.

The ghosts of memories
followed me upstairs and then into bed.
Suddenly I saw all of them,
those who went before me and remembered them.

My mother, would I be cared for like that again?
The child I lost, would I want so intensely again?
My uncle's magic bag, would I feel such joy again?

Bob and jokes, would I laugh that hard again?
Mr. Maier standing amidst the beauty of nature,
would I share a silent communion like that again?

The memories surrounded me.
Remembering, I thanked all of them for their love.
As I closed my eyes, I whispered,
"Yes, I remembered the dead today; my heart is full."

Phyllis Babbs
Harwood Heights, IL

[Hometown] Harwood Heights, IL; [Ed] life; [Occ] full-time Nana, part-time writer; [Hobbies] reading, crossword puzzles; [GA] celebrating fiftieth wedding anniversary

Every word I write is dedicated to the memory of Albert Catalano, my uncle. He taught me the power of words. As a person who was illiterate, he always told me, "If you can read, the whole world is open to you." Thanks, Unckie.

My Friend

Starshine reflects pinpoints of light in the dark pools of the firmament. Speckled and beautiful they are a fine example of our Creator's handy work. Yet with all of this one could not so much as bring a penny in exchange. The transition is impossible. Many of our own greatest deeds of mercy and acts of kindness are fragile and priceless. But again their value cannot be seen nor measured.

As frozen water, ice is brackish and does not reflect well. This is like our hearts when we follow the ways of the world and its desires. Expensive adornment can be worn to become beautiful. Yet nothing matches the magnificence of our very own God our Creator. What truly is the value of our Lord's priceless beauty and grace? To the world we are worthless but to our God our value is matchless beyond compare... even as moonlight.

As God's children each of us are like these pinpoints of light in that great pool of darkness... the world we live in. God has selected us to abide with him in his newly created grand new Earthly kingdom coming down from Heaven. God's only Son is precious and beautiful and none can count the cost of His sacrifice for us. He will reign over the whole earth in Glorious Majesty. Who could place a value? Not a one could bid and win... not a one!

Sandra B. Tremblay
Plattsburgh, NY

[Hometown] Plattsburgh, NY; [DOB] June 22, 1956; [Ed] two-year college degree; [Occ] file clerk; [Hobbies] reading, biking and computer classes; [GA] to be published by you

Carnage

If sports serve as religion for few
In vast numbers, gun lovers worship too
Most of these stay under control
It's the mental defect who shows.
War-like weapons share the blame
as serial killers leave us aflame
but who would loom so bold
to rein in the laws of gun control.
Evil lurks and spews all around
sadly, with anguish, we point to Newtown
A maniac shooting and killing children
stings the soul of all us Pilgrims
in this noble land of plenty—
unthinkable for even one, much less twenty.
A sickness conflicts the killer's brain
outwardly sane, he's driven by pain
He never wonders what's to gain
by rushing out as another Cain.
The big fight goes on—pros and cons,
Pro-gun defending the Constitution
but when—and if—a new era dawns
could we have misread this institution?
How far will the carnage go?
It's in the hands of citizenry to know.

Paul Richard Jordan
Bardstown, KY

[Hometown] Wayland, KY; [DOB] April 1, 1926; [Ed] AB degree in journalism; [Occ] journalist, state and federal government; [Hobbies] photography; [GA] living to eighty-seven

I graduated from Wayland High School and served in Patton's U.S. 3rd Army in Europe during World War II. I wrote my first poetry at the University of Kentucky, where I earned a degree in journalism in 1950. In a literature class, the teacher assigned us to write a Shakespearean sonnet, and I stayed up all night writing one. When sonnets were returned to the students, the teacher had written on mine, "Is this original?" After class, I somewhat indignantly assured her I was the author. She said, "It seems I've read this somewhere before." In a haughty way, I said, "Thanks for the compliment," and I walked away. I went on to become a newspaperman for twelve years, ten years with the Associated Press, and then worked as a public servant in the state and federal government.

He Doesn't Care for Me

He doesn't care for me, I know...
He only wants to spread his wings
And fly away, his freedom holds
The peace of mind he wants to achieve...
For I was told: he doesn't care for me,
I know...

He wants to hold my body closed
And steal the passion I can give.
He wants my body and leaves my soul
Abandoned, lonely, without the affection that it needs...
He doesn't care for me,
I know...

And then, if nothing he can feel,
Let him depart, to others take the road.
Without love my heart cannot persist
Lighting the passion that my body holds...

Susan L. Aragon
Pasadena, CA

Love is the major force that can move our spirits and fill our bodies with wonderful emotions. But there is nothing more devastating than expecting affection from someone who has no feeling for us. Sooner or later we have to accept that a relationship without love has no future.

The Cross

He receives the cross of his own weakness
   and laments its struggle in onerous labor;
Days destined to be filled with tormented fear
   of long dark nights of thankless, reckless savor.

Such contradictions do fill this human heart,
   such folly are his careless deeds intended;
Coursing o'er overwhelming responsibilities
   that fall into categories left unattended.

Prayer, sacrifices, had become his chosen lot—
   at priestly ordination he chastened this vow;
No excuses allowed for slackening aspirations
   though procrastinations dare consume him now.

The aggrieved reality leaves no inner solitude
   as emptiness overcomes the void with pain;
Yet, faith-filled promises of a pious, discerning mind
   render the piercing, compassioned cross its own gain.

Anna Louise Greenmun
Phoenix, AZ

This poem was written during a time of painful turmoil for this young priest. While loving him, no one could ease the confusion that seems to be consuming him. Since I was a teenager (now eighty-one), my poems are from the heart of one who has always felt compassion for those in need. It is the only way I know of expressing this connection.

Return

Love can be like a spider web—for when you're in, you're caught!

Her love, like a woven trap is before my eyes;
But even as I open both eyes wide—
Standing before me, what mysteries lie?
The glow about her,
Insights me as if a radiant energy hovers
To cover my fading, yet current life.
But I struggle not to recover
As my breath becomes breathless, more or less.
For I have crossed over the line, I confess,
Into her mysteries of the unknown,
And my pursuing heart purrs a friendly tone—
Becoming speechless, I groan!
As my behavior topples without pleas…
I step into her web of no return.

Robert Thorpe
Magnolia, TX

[Hometown] Magnolia, TX; [DOB] August 13, 1943; [Ed] high school and college; [Occ] retired from Kraft Foods; [Hobbies] writing poetry; [GA] being married to my wife, Connie Thorpe

My tongue is the pen of a ready writer created by my love to write. This is my soul divider that discloses the motives of my heart, revealing thoughts so that my words are words like those of a poet's ode, a lyric poem more imaginative than ordinary speech—for it's all about the love of writing.

The Special Tree

Of all the trees that please our eye
The one we cut with the most care,
The one that brings the most joy,
Is the one that stands above the toys.
We light it with the glow of lamps;
We hang tinsel from every branch.

We put a huge tree in the square
And make sure Santa's there.
The joy that's seen on infants' faces
Radiates to other places.
This tree God made just right,
And made especially for one night.
On the top we put a "star"
Because that's where our spirits are.

Richard F. Kenney
Coronado, CA

[Hometown] Coronado, CA; [DOB] March 2, 1920; [Ed] military pilot; [Occ] USAF; [Hobbies] skiing, fly fishing; [GA] DFC, Air Medal with 11 OLC, two purple hearts, technical delegate for FIS

I am a ninety-three-year old survivor of WWII, prisoner of war in Germany in WWII, and a career fighter pilot that commanded five fighter squadrons. I am carrier qualified and an honorary Mexican Air Force pilot. I wrote poems for Christmas cards for many years until I ran out of inspiration and ability to print addresses to send them.

Transcendental Spirit

I am not ascendant to any one thing;
Neither poet nor poem—
Song or rhyme.
I write words and dance their rhyme,
Yet not in expression of one species
Or time.

I sing and dance of all ages—
Races: Moses, Genghis Kahn, Alexander,
Napoleon…

I am the four winds that temper the fire of
Hell; the oceans that ebb and swell.

I am the Heavenly elements;
Earth that guides the feet,
Fire that flames passion,
Water that quenches the Soul's thirst, and
Air bringing messages from boundless
Galaxies—populating the uncharted Universe…

I am essence

Mel Scott
Buffalo, NY

[Hometown] West Hollywood, CA; [DOB] March 1; [Occ] actor, singer, dancer, and writer; [Hobbies] astrology-numerology studies; [GA] principal actor on Broadway with Rod Steiger

"Transcendental Spirit" is a metaphysically spiritual poem inspired by a series of dreams and meditations I had logged over time. I struggled to find a character, so to speak, but failed; it was a Force that guided the events, and I ended up riding on its coattail to learn that the universe is in quest of peace, unity and equality.

Let Live

So many hungry hands
In a land of plenty
So many desperate souls

Where, where is everyone going?
What, what do they desire?

A kiss in the dark
A coin in pocket
A moment of fame
We've all been ... this way

I look in
I see my own sins
This is life

Our nomadic beings
Our dreamy thoughts
Our searching souls

All wanting happiness
I only wish I had more to give

Let live
Let live

Rose M. Hick
Santa Rosa, CA

I wish to tell you who I am. I am variegated. I am different colors at different times. I am a camellia. I excel in one area—this area crosses many fields. I touch many people from all walks of life. I hear and see many people, places and things. I live with much amazement and miracles. I am also touched by many. So, life is a two-way street with streaking cars. My main joy is laughter and fun. They come along occasionally, and I cherish every moment. In my true heart is a profound responsibility for survivability and the entertainment of humanity.

Treasury

The country—defend the nation with diamonds
Treasure of the nation full of jewelry
From precious stones, find from mother and
And build a worldwide collection
Defend the nation full of beautiful women
Treasure her the same as Mother Nature
Her pride is rooted in the Virgin Mary
Her dress is designed with style of the land
Pearls on her neck, as if she is the treasure of the ocean
Motherhood creates the image of caregiver
For her man who stands beside her
His handsomeness illuminates her world
Creating a force of nature of mankind
He, who stands tall for his trust
On a journey of space-exploration
Beyond Earth he goes with his pride
To lift up mankind in spirit
To think beyond the narrow path
But the world goes beyond
The imagination of one who has seen
The door of opportunity
For mankind to explore
The opportunity for new generations
To take on the stand of their father's path

Vi Nguyen
Portland, OR

[Hometown] Portland, OR; [DOB] April 4, 1980; [Ed] BS in physics from Portland State University; [Occ] retail manager; [Hobbies] writing song lyrics and poems

I was born in Baothi, Vietnam in 1980 to a Catholic family. My family and I went to the USA in 1993. I pursued a BS in physics at Portland State University in 2004. I got inspired to write this poem from a chance I had to visit Washington, DC, the US Capital and museum in 1998 through a "Close Up" program at James Madison High School. The nation of pride in mankind space exploration inspired me most.

Trifling

You're just a victim of circumstances
You're in and out of failed romances
You feel everyone should give you money
Because you're sure you are everyone's honey
To bail you out, you have everyone rifling
Frankly, my dear, you're just trifling!

Primo
Alexandria, VA

Mercy's Spring

Mercy's spring is flowing freely
Salvation's river to traverse
Grace of God abounding ever
In the shadow of His love

Step we then into that river
Fed by springs from God's own throne
Eternal life abounding ever
Granted by the Savior's blood

Meet us there, my Savior always
Living Water manifest
Takes my hand as I step into Him
Leads me to eternal rest

Shannon McCarville
Chester, AR

Epitaph of Sherri Jensen

Here lies Sherri Jensen,
Her person is full of zest,
All wondered at the simplistic life
Which brought her happiness,
What drove her on through rocky-paths,
Some can only guess,
But those observing knew her sorrows
Meaningful
Her joys unsurpassed.
The flowers strewn behind her path were
Plucked by passers-by
And used through generations present
And past
For heartfelt exercise.

Sherri B. Jensen
Sandy, UT

[Hometown] Sandy, UT; [DOB] September 28, 1922; [Ed] two semesters college, business and Shakespeare English; [Occ] housewife, secretary, artist, and med. water colors; [Hobbies] water colors, parent reading, acting, poetry, art, and writing; [GA] receiving second and third art contest awards, poetry, Eber & Wein calling me a poet!

I have just turned ninety years of age. I have found it to be enjoyable. I am in fair health and very positive about the future. I feel that I shall see my family and be united. I have no morbid feelings about my passing on. I want my family to feel happy as I am happy! Hence, "Epitaph of Sherri Jensen"! I am presently taking care of myself and invalid husband who is ninety-three years old.

A Day of Rain

Though I never knew a Newtown soul
My heart is carrying a heavy toll
Little angels gone in the blink of an eye
Taken by a past, which wouldn't die
How could one create so much pain
See tears of loss now fall like rain
Where was compassion and the gift of love
Each newborn carries from up above
Precious and innocent, we come one and all
What lessons were taught, which created the fall
Love begets love, pain begets pain
One's pain-filled lessons create future rain
We are all connected, though it's not widely known
Loveless actions reap the sad seeds sown
So guard each action with a guiding light
Teach children of love with all your might
We need little angels here with us on Earth
Their lives, the greatest gift of value and worth
Time and forgiveness will start to heal, but never forget
Acts against angels and a day God wept

Steve Opper
Metamora, IL

[Hometown] Washington, IL; [DOB] April 8, 1957; [Ed] BA in management; [Occ] journeyman, lineman; [Hobbies] skiing, chess, staying fit; [GA] gaining presence

I hope this poem allows people to self-reflect on how we are all partly responsible for the societies we live within!

The Immigrant

They came from far and distant lands,
For a better life and their fortunes to seek;
The only skills they brought were their strong backs and hands
And their future, I'm sure, must have at times looked bleak.

But these pioneers were of a hardy and enduring stock,
And hard work was not foreign to them at all.
They cleared the virgin land of forest, swamp and rock,
And farmed the land and cut the pine tree tall.

But a far greater wealth of mineral lay beneath the ground...
And an ever-expanding steel industry would soon need it all.
These miners then began mining the iron ore that was found;
Their numbers were multiplied as others came to industry's call.

They built the cities, towns and hamlets that soon dotted the countryside,
And an ethnic heritage of hard-working and law-abiding people was left behind
To which their offspring and future generations could point with pride
And say, These were our forbearers and the land that they mined.
A nation's strength is only as strong as its people,
And these indomitable ancestors were truly a model for us all:
A God-fearing and hard-working people whose wants were simple.
May we all be humbled by their courage, trials and ordeals...lest we fall.

Steve Chicka
New Berlin, WI

[Hometown] New Berlin, WI; [DOB] September 4, 1921; [Ed] high school, two-year college graduate; [Occ] retired driver/salesperson; [Hobbies] being inducted into the National Honor's Society in high school

I am a retired World War II veteran who served three and a half years in the Army Air Corp. I love to read and write poetry. My poems have been published in numerous books by Eber & Wein and I want to thank them for that. Poetry to me is a story put to verse. I wrote this poem as a tribute to those early pioneers who came to northern Minnesota to work in the iron ore mines in Hibbing, MN.

Retirement

Remember all the years you worked
   and couldn't wait to be retired?
It's not what it's cut out to be,
   it leaves a lot to be desired.

Wait 'til you buy medicine,
   a prescription for your ills.
Whenever something's just not right,
   the doctor gives you pills.

There's never enough money
   because you get no weekly check.
Compared to the salary you used to earn
   your retirement is just a speck.

The aches and pains as you grow old
   will really bring you down.
The friendly smile you used to have
   will be turned into a frown.

I feel like I am beaten up
   And it makes me want to sob.
Instead of this retirement,
   I'd rather have a job!

Thomas Bennett
Byron, IL

I was a police officer and police sergeant for several police departments, a security chief for a private organization and a deputy coroner in the state of Illinois for a total of about thirty years. A heart attack in 2007 then a full hip replacement and four other hip-related surgeries in 2011 forced me into retirement. Even though I am currently sixty-three years old, I am very unhappy being unable to work in my chosen profession, which motivated me to write this poem about retirement.

Trusting

I never told you that I trusted
you from the first time I saw you.
I think that if I had been older
than nineteen or that you were not just
starting medical school, I
might have not felt confused
or that I was being backed into a corner;
you knew about my childhood and
the shattered feelings that I had.
Even though you gave me over two years
of teaching me about being cared about
and how to return those feelings,
I always knew what you thought
about me and that you loved me.
I just wish that I could have had
more time to trust everything that was
being pushed at me as I felt
I was being backed into what
seemed an inescapable corner.
If I had we would be alive
and together or dead from the
car accident that took you from me.
Either way I would have learned
about trusting and believing thirty-nine
years sooner.

Vickie Hannawell
Beloit, WI

[Hometown] Janesville, WI; [DOB] July 13, 1954; [Ed] BA social work; [Occ] disabled; [Hobbies] writing, reading, quilting, counted cross-stitch; [GA] being a mother

I write because it helps to slow down my thinking. It also helps to put the past in the past and allows things happening now to stay in the now. I also write because I have always enjoyed it since I learned how to do it. I find it's easier to express my feelings to people in writing.

The Scandal Sheets

I like to read the scandal sheets
To see what's going on.
When people see me reading them
They think my brain is gone.
But you don't know the many things
That they reveal to me.
I'm like the queen of England
With my jolly company!
If I live to be one hundred
I'll be a paranormal then.
And I can live rent free
In the same old house again.
My neighbors will be aliens.
I can always fade.
House work will be a piece
of cake.
How much dust can an old
ghost make?

Doris Insero
Schenectady, NY

[Hometown] Schenectady, NY; [DOB] January 10, 1934; [Ed] high school; [Occ] WMHT membership; [Hobbies] writing songs, TV, reading; [GA] my poetry

I'm a seventy-nine-year-old widow who lives with her sister in Schenectady, NY. I was a high school dropout but went on to take courses that enabled me to hold many responsible jobs. I have been writing songs since I was a child.

Seek His Face with Patience

We pray to God each day with care
    with faith we know that God is there!
We might think that it's out of sight
    but He answers us when the time is right.

We long to hear His voice divine
    and see His garments, oh so fine
His eyes, His hair, and smiling face
    the Lord of love and amazing grace.

To kiss His hand would be so sweet
    or rubbing oil on His feet.
To hug Him, this my love would show
    but then I might not let Him go.

Lord on high in the holy place
    someday we'll see Him face to face.
And kneel before the Heavenly Host
    our Father, Son, and Holy Ghost!

For now I'll pray and with patience wait
    to someday meet Him at the gate.
And when it happens bells will chime
    when God says, "Come son now's the time."

Donald B. Perlinger
North Huntingdon, PA

I praise God for all my victories no matter where or how I obtain them. Poetry is a blessing that Jesus gave me as a gift! So I give him all the credit. All my poems are inspired by God and my love for him gives me a good subject to write about. My hope as a believer in Jesus is that the words of this poem will happen to me in this manner when my days on this Earth are over. Thank You, Jesus!

Dinner in Paris

As they crossed the threshold silence filled the room.
She was beautiful and he magnificent.
They were shown to the table
by a window that overlooked the Seine.
She was seated and he sat close to her.
She leaned over and whispered in his ear
while rubbing the back of his neck.
When wine was served her glass was filled,
she touched his chin indicating not for him.
Dinner arrived; she had Dover Sole,
he a large T-bone steak.
She would often reach over and lovingly touch him.
Eyes followed their every move;
low murmurs made a soft humming sound.
As they were leaving one of the guests reached out
but did not touch her and asked,
"Who are you?"
She smiled and told her her name, turned and said,
"This is Wellington my Weimaraner."

Patricia M. Bisgrove
Brookings, OR

[Hometown] Panama, Canal Zone; [DOB] December 10, 1941; [Ed] BS education; [Occ] retired teacher; [Hobbies] photography; [GA] winning third place in poetry international

I've published three books of poetry, two children's books, and two whimsical books on photos of driftwood, twice winning third place in poetry international competition. My poetry has been published in books and magazines. I have been in Who's Who in Poetry for a number of years. This summer my photos received an award and a grant from the Brookings Art Festival, a juried art show conducted in Oregon.

Bridge: Fantasia Finesse

When the Ace of trumps falters in favor
Then the Queen of hearts becomes frustrated
So then the bidding is instituted in no trump.

When an Ace of trumps needs stable support
Then the King, Queen and Jack must be in attendance
 So the trumping support is two-to-thirteen.

When the Ace has a number count of four
Then the King has a number count of three
And the Queen has a number count of two
So the Jack has a number count of one.

When the rank and file are filled in line
Then the order in power is the same as such
So they are Clubs, Diamonds, Hearts and Spades
And when the bidding in the King of Clubs is increasing.

When grand slam is all thirteen playing books
Then six playing books is mandatory of two partners
So the beginning bid is over the six mandatory books.

When reading bridge play in the Midwest press
Then the card deal is stacked in favor of North and South
So very seldom is East or West to become a champion
This also the card-playing, bridge beginner
And card-playing is a person of an observer
Making mistakes is in the odd's favor
Therefore, betting the home ranch is not recommended
But betting small monetary change increases the interest

Ronald L. Libengood
Colorado Springs, CO

[Hometown] Erie, PA; [DOB] December 31, 1940; [Ed] two college semesters of English and business management; [Occ] disabled veteran; [Hobbies] motorcycles, woodworking; [GA] thirty years of marriage

Why?

Why are we here?
Why should I care?
One hundred years give or take will slowly disappear.
Where do we go?
We're here to grow.
Grow and fade away like the melting snow.
Do we influence?
Make a difference?
Will anyone remember us anyway?
How far is space?
What is this place?
Are we cosmic astronauts in a celestial place?
Is God the start?
Is heaven part
Of the creation story or just within my heart?
How can we exist?
How can we resist
Fables and folklore , doctors and scientist.
Preachers and the faithful,
Lawyers and politics,
Religion and believers, deities and Atheist.
Is there one God?
One earth on which to trod?
One planet of living species in one tiny little pod?
I can not comprehend.
Save me!
Show me!
Help me understand.

Mark Darretta
Cape May Court House, NJ

I am a fifty-two-year-old, self-made poet and philosopher with three grown children and two stepchildren. I am retired from law enforcement and through my experiences in the field, have found life and people to be complex. I am a Christian and believe in Christ Jesus as my savior but that hasn't left me any more satisfied with the question of our existence. Even though I believe God is the creator, I still ponder where he came from. I also cannot comprehend time and space and matter continuing on for infinity. You can literally blow your mind trying to put your head around it. Live life and enjoy your family and do good unto others. That's all I can say. Personally, I continue to believe in God and I trust when I die there will be a heaven and a place of eternal paradise.

Found Again

lost my mind lost myself
lost people and things
felt like nothing
nothing mattered
grew tired and weak
heart felt dying
saw my thoughts to be true
was a long trip
'til I tripped over myself
woke up to reality
decided to live
among the living
realized it was me
that I had to be the one
to walk in these shoes
and to believe that I was not alone

Vanessa Lemieux
Edmonton, AB Canada

[Hometown] Fort McMurray, AB; [DOB] May 4, 1976; [Ed] college; [Occ] artist; [Hobbies] painting, writing

My poem reflects my battle with my mental illness, schizophrenia. I have been sick since I was seventeen. I release my feelings into my paintings and my poetry. Doing this makes me happy to be myself.

The Man on the Moon

He's the man on the moon who holds out his hand;
he pulls me up through the stars, onto a new land.
He is the king there, and he makes all the laws,
he takes me to a lake to wash away all my flaws.
He wraps me in his arms and says to hold on tight,
and that he's not done till the end of the night.
We drop into a castle where he's a wizard-to-be,
So he lifts up his wand to erase my memory.
With his hand around my waist, he whispers, "Just one more thing."
I hover down and let him take me under his wing.
We land in a closet, with brand new clothes for me;
and after I change, there's something he wants me to see.
He pulls me towards him and says, "Open your eyes"...
And there was a mirror, full of lies.
My appearance so perfect, and my past now erased,
I was a porcelain doll, completely fake.
I burst out in tears and begged to go back,
but he told me he wouldn't love me like that.
He said it was time for me to face reality,
that someone like him could never love the real side of me.
I opened my eyes to myself in my bed...
The "man of my dreams" was all in my head.
When I looked in the mirror,
I was happy to see
that nothing had changed—
I was looking at the real me, and I always will be.

Kathleen Mary Sandstrom
Rocky Point, NY

[Hometown] Rocky Point, NY; [DOB] February 7, 1994; [Ed] college student; [Occ] student of psychology; [Hobbies] reading, writing, drawing; [GA] first time being published

I wrote this poem when I found myself, when I realized who I really am. Knowing who you are, believing in who you are, and loving who you are will be key points in living a long, joyful and successful life.

Make No Mistake

I am not a precious jewel,
nor a fragile piece of glass,
not just a treasure here
for you to take
and hide away in your cache.

I am not a gilded bauble,
nor a pretty little pearl,
not some adornment here
for you to buy
and show in pride to the world.

I am not a valued gemstone,
nor a cherished possession
not an ornament here
for you to see
and make an obsession.

And make no mistake
about that.

Madison Ramos
Wapato, WA

[Hometown] Wapato, WA; [DOB] October 10, 1995; [Ed] EV online learning; [Occ] student; [Hobbies] reading, baking; [GA] has yet to be achieved

Forgive Me?

I'm really so sorry
And feel so very sad
I did miss your birthday
How could I be so bad?

Just 'cause I have false teeth
And need my hearing aids
Should I accept the fact
That status *"old"* I've made?

I love living my life
And party when I'm asked
I frown at "body pains"
That "age" hides in its mask

But all this does not help
To take my guilt away
Of what I did to you
An awful thing, I'd say

It's really all my fault
Because "my brain" forgot
If you'll forgive this time
Next year, *"forget"* I'll not!

Marlene R. Murrell
Calimesa, CA

[Hometown] Cincinnati, OH; [DOB] June 28, 1931; [Ed] high school graduate; [Occ] retired from forty years with air force civil service; [Hobbies] writing poetry and hopeful to publish a book; [GA] early years was a professional horseback rider in horse shows and have written poetry since the 1960s

After high school graduation, I went to work at Wright Patterson Air Base in Dayton, OH until the age of twenty-seven when I was transferred out to California to work in the SAMSO (Space and Missile Systems Organization) in 1958. I remained with civil service for an additional forty years until retirement. I was very dedicated to my job and proud to say I worked my way up from a GS-1 to a GS-11 chief of billeting before retirement. It was some time in the 1960s that I was in a supervisory position in which people would come to me to write recommendations or farewell words or promotion words to and for employees who were being transferred or leaving the organization. I cannot explain how or why, but these words I began writing all seemed to just turn out as rhymes that ended up sounding like short stories telling of the people and their work. Ever since then, I've been writing rhyming poems for every subject imaginable.

The Joys of Life

Walking along the beach
Making sure he is in my reach
Little footprints in the sand
As he grabs ahold of my hand
The love I have for him is unknown
Can't believe how much he has grown
Finding seashells, saying Mommy, come look!
From day one, that little boy had my heart took
We'd play in the water with a big splash
Or go fishing and he'd be the one with the first catch
He's my everything, my heart
I hope we're never apart
The smile on his face makes my day
In all my life, I wouldn't want this feeling to ever go away

Jessica Lynn Knight
Clinton, SC

[Hometown] Clinton, SC; [DOB] December 6, 1988

My goal in life is to give my all to my kids. I am blessed to be here and thank God every day. I'm a disabled stay-at-home mom, and I am truly blessed.

Whispered Prophecy

I now know,
Nothing here will last.
And so,
I fashion poems
From fragments of the past:
A world in pieces,
My inner eye must reassemble,
My heart's odd logic reconstruct.
But both filter truth,
And I trust them not.

For the river of my life
Passes more swiftly now,
And whispers:
"Prepare for journeys yet ahead.
Soon you shall behold
The splendor and the wonder
Ancient tales have long foretold,
Of worlds beyond
This planet's familiar shore.
Your heart shall know
The truth of stars,
And long for Earth no more."

Patric Baylis-André
Ocala, FL

[Hometown] Philippine Islands; [DOB] 1922; [Ed] BFA, master's in education; [Occ] artist; [Hobbies] music, history, and literature; [GA] having my paintings exhibited with the inauguration of Venezuela's first Museum of Modern Art: Caracas 1956

Living and working as the artist "Patric" in Mexico, Pat exhibited internationally, most notably at the inauguration of Museum of Modern Art, Caracas '56 and International World's Fair, Brussels '58. Moving to the Yucatan in 1968 as the artist in residence at historic Hacienda Chichen-Itza, Patric created a technique for temple rubbings transforming huge Mayan monuments into a more practical and accessible art form. Returning to the U.S. after forty-seven years abroad, Patric now resides in Ocala, FL and recently served as a juror for Infinity Art Galleries online "Exhibit '09" featuring artists from around the world by computer.

To Love a Tigress

She appeared at the disco out of the mist
We danced a while and then we kissed
Like hunted tigress she played the game,
She turned out not to be so tame,
Love was my one and only feeling
Bad lady luck she wasn't dealing
I chased her for weeks but with no joy
She was the cat and I was her joy
Although she was always close by
One day I seemed to catch her eye
With panting breath and pounding heart
I moved in closer to play my part
She knew my every single thought
'Twas just then the tigress I caught
A girl with looks, she was a dream
Just as nice as peaches and cream
Now the relationship began to flourish
Me with the tigress I would always cherish
Many days and nights we lived as one
Soon the partnership was full of fun
We laughed, and played, we talked and talked
And decided to marry one day while we walked
Forty years later, we're still full of laughter
It's fair to say, we lived happily ever after.

Anthony Baker
Clearwater, FL

[Hometown] Clearwarter, FL; [DOB] November 11, 1939; [Ed] physical training instructor; [Occ] retired; [Hobbies] building models from match sticks; [GA] singing to two thousand people on a cruise ship

Please Whisper

Please whisper all your dreams to me
For I love you without question
My heart, your gentle soul I will keep
Tucked softly within my heart
I know you long for me, to be with you
To hold you tight, while you cry
Hold you tight, while you sigh
To be a part of your life, without lies
Whisper gently into my ear this day
For I long to hear all your pleas
I carry you in my heart, with care
Allowing your soul, to speak to me
But yet, to be free
To be with you, and you with me
That is what would please me
Your whispers in the night
Through the day
Into the future with me

Ramona Quivonia Prak
El Cajon, CA

[Hometown] El Cajon, CA; [DOB] October 16, 1954; [Occ] teacher's aide for twenty-five years, childcare for fifteen years, and author; [GA] published "The Legend of Blue Eagle"

"Please Whisper" is about my longing for a love that was also in my life many years ago. He is the one that got away and the one that I most likely will never have. I place all that in God's hands, for I want him to have what he desires: God's blessings, love, grace, happiness and to look forward to a life filled with hope. I am content within myself and my love for God and His choices to come first. Life is too short to not be happy with the one you are supposed to love.

The Rope

I'm at the bottom of a deep pit,
The walls of which are incredibly smooth.
Confusion, frustration and anger
Make up the walls of this pit.
I'm so far down, I can't see the top.
The way to get out is a single rope—
The rope is made of understanding.
It is anchored to the rock of compassion;
The light by which you can find the rope
Is made of therapy and meds.
Without the light, you remain lost,
Unable to find the way out.
The climb is long and arduous.
At times, you may slip back down.
The pit is not a fun place to be…
Voices call out to you, no one else hears them,
You see things no one else sees,
You eat less and sleep more,
You feel alone, as if there
Is no one else in the world.
You trust no one and cling
To the past.
Yet, you desperately want to get out of the pit.
That is depression from the inside.

Frederic Wiggins
Lumberton, NC

[Hometown] Lumberton, NC; [DOB] January 26, 1955; [Ed] Virginia Military Institute; [Occ] herbalist; [Hobbies] stamp collecting, making collage pictures

What has stimulated most of my poetry is the loss of my fiancée. She died of a ruptured brain aneurysm, a week before our wedding. Depression has fueled many of my poems. They tend to make people feel sad upon reading them. Hopefully, I'll get over this, sooner or later. I have almost fallen for other women, but I still feel like I'm cheating on my fiancée. I know better, but my mind still jumps to that conclusion.

Heart of Mine

Sanded toes, winded heart
Tide in, its beauty mark
Arms across, holds me tight
Reflection of the sun, the warm light
Bubbles... ripples... wondrous underneath
Gazing, grasping, through the eyes I see
Yellow purple, blue, and pink
The beautiful colors, to sea I sink
Holding my passion, never-ending hopes
Giving my heart, and the mind I hold
Brushing slowly, moving along
Dreaming of reality as I write this song
Asleep... peace... mind free
Fantasy, beauty, make believe
In reality, dreamland made
I live here, in hopes for pray
As I wake, to match the same
For the finish line to appear, the devil's game
Peeking through, sun shined
I release, I give... this heart of mine

Paige Anderson
Kenosha, WI

[Hometown] Kenosha, WI; [DOB] May 20, 1992; [Ed] graduated high school, enrolling in college for liberal arts, eventually zoology; [Occ] on disability, full-time mommy, barn work; [Hobbies] hiking, being at the ranch with my horse, riding, exploring; [GA] my daughter

I am a proud full-time mommy of a beautiful daughter, with a love for the rehabilitation of many animals, but most of all, being connected at the soul with my own rescue horses, which made more dreams come true. All my animals, family and love make me whole. I love being outdoors. Amongst many passions, what inspires me, writing poetry, will always remain.

My True Best Friend

A friend is someone who is always there
In my time of need
Helping any way they can
Without acknowledgment of the deed

They won't ask for any payment
As assistance is freely given
And never keeps track of favors
As their intentions are heartfelt driven

The ultimate friend would give their life
To save mine in the end
I do believe I would have to say
This type of love, only God can send

There is only one I can count on
Until the very end
Yes, that would be my Lord and Savior
Who is truly my best friend

Deanna Lynn Walton
Spring Grove, PA

[Hometown] Hanover, PA; [DOB] June 29; [Ed] high school and trade school; [Occ] medical transcriber; [Hobbies] reading, crocheting; [GA] being a supervisor/legal liaison for eighteen years

I am the middle daughter of three girls, whose mother stayed at home, and influenced me with poetry, music and the arts. Dad was a hardworking man, instilling a strong work ethic, as well as faith and moral values. A combination of family, friends and acquaintances, along with health issues, loss of loved ones and daily challenges of life contribute to my poetry. Now residing in a small town in Pennsylvania, I had lived in Baltimore, MD for a few years, but always have gravitated back to a rural setting, as that is where my heart truly resides.

Where Trees Since Fallen

"Cometh out from under 'tis moss, of darkness and rot
where trees have since fallen, upon branches twisted at knot
Crawleth away through deepest forest, its trails left behind
shadowed over haggard troddened heaps, perished in time

Straighteneth burdeneth knees, gaze amidst the ground
cast distance upon distance, where vine crawleth to surround
Now thrust its decay away from thy face
arise now on touch feet, to leave thine terrible place

As thou art standing, take cast around
listen for whispers, nothing approacheth thee, but beautiful sounds
Harbor a full breath, stride the clearset of trees
surrender thy gaze upwards, for 'tis I, thy Saviour, abiding over thee

Halt now in sunlight, let thine heart inherit this gift
inhale a sweet savor of rose smell, I now send swift
Follow thine heart and step o'er step, from where thou art
for I have now opened a winged pathway, a safely depart.

Barbara Kim Stump
Parkersburg, WV

*[Hometown] Parkersburg, WV; [DOB] August 24, 1960; [Ed] high school; [Hobbies] poet laureate/visual
jewelry; [GA] being saved by my Lord and having my children*

Perfection

The sky is glowing this beautiful day
Birds are singing and squirrels are at play
The trees are swaying in the breeze
And everything's doing as they please.

What a glorious day to be alive
Enjoying nature from nine to five
And to all who enjoy a sunset view
This poem is connecting me to you.

God makes the heavens really bright
And our thanks are given every night
For the beauty that surrounds us every day
Whether we work or take time to play.

Mae Levaas
Fort Myers, FL

[Hometown] Apollo, PA; [DOB] October 5, 1927; [Ed] high school and on-the-job training; [Occ] retired supervisor at Telco; [Hobbies] gardening, traveling; [GA] my two wonderful sons

I live on a beautiful canal in Florida, and the turtles come right up to my dock when they see me there. I toss pieces of bread to them and sometimes count up to fifteen turtles munching away. I also have a huge oak tree in my yard, which is home to many squirrels; they take peanuts off a stick I hold up to them.

Death Is Not a Thing to Fear

Death is not a thing to fear
You shouldn't be afraid
If you give your soul to Jesus
Your debt in life's been paid
Once upon a time
A long, long time ago
Sin was an unforgivable crime
To hell you would go
But God is full of mercy
God is number one
God so loved us, everyone
He gave for us His only Son
Jesus conquered death
Jesus is Life
Death is not a thing to fear
Jesus paid the price
Jesus walked through hell for us
His suffering was immense
Death is not a thing to fear
Use your common sense
Jesus awaits our arrival in Heaven
His love for us sincere
Death is only Heaven's departure
Death is not a thing to fear.

Kevin E. Helms
Pittsburg, KS

[Hometown] Kansas City, MO; [DOB] November 12, 1963; [Ed] high school diploma; [Occ] disabled; [Hobbies] writing poems, lyrics, watching sports, movies, traveling; [GA] accepting Jesus as my Lord and Savior

Being a poet/lyricist ranks with the greatest gifts God has bestowed upon me. I began writing seriously on September 12, 1986, penning "Nothing Will Keep Us Apart" (a song). It is my hope to touch as many hearts as I can via my writings. Ultimately, I'd love to publish my combined writings in a book titled, One Man's Heart. I love being a poet/lyricist and being able to touch people's hearts and hopefully make a difference. I thank God wholeheartedly for this gift. Thank you for reading my poem. May God bless and prosper you, always.

The Mountains

The mountains tall and majestic
Hold your attention as you go.
The view from far or near is fantastic,
Appealing to every eye you know.
Mountains with pine, fir and aspen
Then on top, barren, and frozen.
Memories linger for the way it has been,
A place to love that many have chosen.
From the mountain we proceed to prairie,
Still high elevation but ranch and farm.
Here a type of ready beauty didn't tarry
But still it has appeal and charm.
Winter is sunny and often so cold
Summer is better for those needing warm.
Visits to this land never get old
A nice place to travel without harm.
Many visitors have come to see
Traffic sometimes gets too heavy,
But still it's a good place to be,
A place to which I could flee.
The Rockies such beauty are given
Appears it has a strong appeal.
It calls to many a man for a place of living.
Come live here, this place is for real.

Larry K. Verley
Boerne, TX

[Hometown] Riverton, WY; [DOB] May 26, 1940; [Ed] MBA; [Occ] retired; [Hobbies] golfing and church ministries; [GA] success in military

Larry Verley was born on his father's homestead in Wyoming in 1940. After a college degree from the University of Wyoming, Larry spent twenty-one years in the US Air Force and earned a master's degree from Michigan State University. He then worked for four different companies until retirement to Texas. This poem was inspired by living near those mountains. I write poetry as an inspired hobby, including to honor someone.

My Colorado Home

Spring has come to the high Rocky Mountains and nature's abundance springs forth.
The Colorado gold rush is here to stay as we are bathed with golden sunshine each and every day.

There is nothing sweeter than to smell the forest, sage grass, and wild flowers, and wheat.
The coveted rain showers clothe the flora with glitter and shiny baubles.

The blue Pasque flower emerges and opens its heart so the sun may nurture its soul.
The Kinnikinnick plant sends its far-reaching arms over the forest floor, then waits for the black bear to come and devour.

The spotted deer fawns stay close to Momma and she does her best to protect them from trauma.
Mother moose teaches her long-legged baby to swim the lake, crying and splashing the entire way.

The Bald Eagle in flight teaches its eaglet to delight in the rainbow trout seen far below.
The Golden Eagle soars and its wings nearly roar as it flies low to see if I am too large to eat.

The night owl calls as the sun finally falls and the elk begins to bugle his song.

When fall does come and the harvest is done, the Blue Jay arrives and cries, "Feed me, feed me!"
Many of the animals now take a rest as there will be a test to weather the long, silent, snowy cold winter.

There is no place I would rather be than in my home in Colorado.

Renae A. Olson
Loveland, CO

[Hometown] Loveland, CO; [DOB] March 26, 1954; [Ed] AA in general education, BS in natural health; [Occ] Technician II, health information; [Hobbies] creativity and the outdoors; [GA] Life-Saving Award

My inspiration for this poem is my beautiful Colorado home. My hobbies include travel, gardening, outdoors, photography and reading. Some of my greatest achievements are that I received a life-saving award from the Epilepsy Foundation, raised a family, continue to work, started publishing my written words and have never turned down the opportunity to continue to learn.

Stuff

I'm drowning in stuff, how much is enough?
Want this, don't want that, need this, don't need that
I go 'round the house and constantly mutter
Why is it so hard to get rid of the clutter?
When did I buy this, what tour was I on?
I don't even know what country it's from
I'm so tired of hearing "Where did you get that?"
You can't have been sober just blind as a bat.

I talked to some cherubs who floated above
But they giggled and said, "We're all about love."
The angels just sighed and folded their wings,
Said, "What makes you think we care about things?"
The saints how they laughed, said, "Why all the fuss?
Surely you know that means nothing to us."
God did not laugh, he looked rather severe,
Said, "What makes you think your stuff belongs here?
And though you may think me rather unkind
You even must leave your bodies behind."

The Devil of course had to have his say
And he slyly said, "Just send it my way."

Leonie F. Nulle
Media, PA

[Hometown] Media, PA; [DOB] August 11, 1918; [Ed] French convent in Belgium; [Hobbies] not cooking; [GA] staying alive

I am ninety-five. During World War II, I lived in London with my family. We heard Winston Churchill on the radio telling us we were at war. At first, going to our jobs was painful and depressing. Everyone looked downcast and gloomy, white-faced and tired. No one smiled. That suddenly changed. There were big guns in all our parks, and at times the noise was deafening—guns firing up and bombs coming down. There were no more grim looks, no more white faces, no more gloom...everyone was smiling! No one wants to be a sitting duck.

Yesterday's Rose

The sun was brilliant yesterday
In its glory
High up in the sky
It surely shone brighter
The more you smiled—
The sky turned bluer to match your eyes
The rose you gave me
Was the prettiest red
That I have ever seen
But then the day was over,
As though it had never been
The sun is still bright,
But without your smile,
its glory is somewhat dimmed
And the bluest sky just can't compare
With the blue that it could have been
But the red is still perfect,
As perfect goes,
And my memories feel real again
When I look at yesterday's rose.

Brenna Beale
Logan, UT

This poem is for Loki, who inspired me to pick up my pen.

Our Friend

Cancer here, cancer there,
cancer everywhere.
Of course, wake up!
It's part of you.

Manipulators win,
inflexibles lose.
They just can't see,
it's part of us.

It heals, it cures,
no other friend,
does more for us.
And you blame cancer?

Juan Angel Trigo
Carolina, Puerto Rico

Divine Connection

Somewhere in my youth,
I dared to explore my little world
Puzzled, bothered, and bewildered,
I looked up to Heaven.

I want to share a part of me,
I knew not how or when,
I see the world in her full glory,
and even all the miseries.

One day in my maturity,
I felt the touch of God,
I then saw the light of wisdom,
that opened up my heart.

Your messages into my pen, Oh Lord,
my writings be read and heard,
My devotion be understood,
for my love to Thy people,
my very soul agree.

Let Your loving touch remain,
So all my thoughts be written,
Now I know how to embrace the world,
Because of this Divine connection.

Aniceta P. Alcayaga
San Diego, CA

[Hometown] Dagupan City, Philippines; [DOB] September 19, 1940; [Ed] collegiate (bachelor of arts); [Occ] certified activity specialist; [Hobbies] gardening, writing, collecting novels; [GA] receiving trophy for my work

I was a working student in college, secretary to the Dean of Education. In between school I work part time in radio as a DJ. I married at the age of twenty-four. I worked full time in radio for twenty-six years and managed the local radio station for three years. Coming to America with my husband I got a job in February 2001, in the activity department in a facility for elderly. I was certified and the thrilling challenges in my job gave me a trophy, one of my greatest achievements. Retired in 2001, I devote myself to my family. My hobbies are gardening, collecting novels, and of course writing poems. I will continue doing this. My family is supportive, my grandchildren, Jenna (nine) and Ian Russell (fifteen), are my young coaches and inspirations in my writings. Thank God I have these connections.

Good Luck

I was in the casino the other night
And I have never gambled.
I sat next to a man who
Apparently wanted to talk
And on and on he rambled.

He told me about his family
His wife
And three bad boys.
He said he had to leave the house
Because of all the noise.

He played the wheel as I looked on.
He bet on number 16.
He missed it once.
No more than twice.
He called the old wheel "Mean!"

He changed his number
Now playing twenty
He played four times in a row.
He lost each time
And finally said, "I guess I'd better go."

I stayed awhile
And thought should I
Try my luck like Drew?
I decided my family of two is sweet.
And I'll return home too.

Winifred Smith Eure
Maplewood, NJ

I, Winifred Smith Eure, grew up in a small New Jersey community by the name of Roselle. I lived there many years until I met the man who became my husband. After receiving a BA degree from Douglass College—Rutgers the State University, NJ and a teaching certificate and an MA degree in special education from Kean University, NJ, I taught in Newark Public Schools for twenty-six years. I enjoy working with young people, writing poetry, occasional dining out, and traveling. I would have to say my greatest achievement was meeting and marrying my compatible husband, Clarence, whom I loved dearly.

Reflection

The eyes are from where comes reflection.
Try not to forget that connection;
for the sky in the windows
and the windows in the mirror
are all the perception
of something not quite so clear.
As you see, the mirror reflecting the windows
and the windows reflecting the sky
are but reflections reflecting
into the lens of each eye.

Michelle Haas
Pittsburgh, PA

Michelle Haas is a mother, writer, and abstract artist residing in Southwestern Pennsylvania. At the age of twenty-one, she earned her associate's degree in psychology. Perplexed with what she would truly enjoy to study, she discontinued college to devote time to a myriad of artistic endeavors. Fascinated by the rhythm of language, Michelle's poem "Reflection" is an expression of how things are not always what they seem. It is her musing: in taking a step back to analyze reflection itself, lies the recognition of the diversity of perception to gain for oneself a broader perspective of all things reflected.

A Search for Truth

Do you hear or do you listen?
Does a diamond shine or does it glisten?
A question always demands an answer
Even as the right shoes fit the right dancer
Memories like an echo of forgotten dreams
Shine with the force of unfaded moonbeams
Human is the voice that speaks
Brave is the heart that conquers
Sunsets are a reflection
Of a world not our own
They speak of colors in the Heavens
Where spirits have flown
And now I long for a touch
Just enough to taste but not too much
Of the magic of spring
And the color of the wind
From dust to desire
The beauty of life is seen
And searching for myself I wonder
Where have I been?

George Benaquista
Belleville, NJ

I am from Belleville, NJ, born January 12. A time traveler, music is my passion. I also like reading. I believe a good book has great power, as someone once quoted. This poem is about searching for self-awareness in a world hard to understand.

Forgetless

In my dream, there was x-ray paper
shimmering iridescent, like the last sunrise
As a raven-haired beauty cupped her hands
on both sides of this wondrous
yet plain papyrus thing
Forgetless was the blue hue
lighting her perfect alabaster face
Meanwhile, I was off to the left side, pondering
possible radiation poisoning's repercussions
As I physically coordinated remote viewing
within the control tower of the netherworld
A chill not only in your spine, but of your very soul
(if you have one)...arose from nowhere
Focused and calm, as one can ever be
And yet, I had not the gumption to cry out
for her to stop!
All around the world, a billion or so similar
scenarios simultaneously played out
That blue energy mesmerized one and all
until the pitch-black void
snuffed it

Troy TMX Maddox
Aransas Pass, TX

[Hometown] Aransas Pass, TX; [DOB] January 1, 1957; [Ed] indigenous worldwide history, art, religion,
culture; [Occ] grinderman, boat propellor repairman, low brow artist, sci-fi poet, modern music aficionado;
[Hobbies] being Reese and Dylan's PawPaw

Heavenly Things

The road of life can be steep and rough
And walking the narrow path is tough
When you've lost your way and wasted time
Loathe to begin yet another climb
It helps to think on heavenly things
Like streets of gold and seraphim wings
Where the heart's true rest is not a dream
And healing trees line the crystal stream

When suffering comes and lays you low
The pain inside too deep to show
Family and friends try to comfort you
But they don't feel what you're going through
It's time to think on heavenly things
Like the peace that trusting God will bring
No more crying alone at night
Where mansions shine with the Lamb of light

Whenever sorrow has its season
Heaven only knows the reason
Remember there's a lovely place
Where our angels see the Father's face
Don't hold anger; let bitterness go
And like our Lord, let forgiveness flow
Pure joy within your soul will spring
When you turn your thoughts to heavenly things

Josette Nilles Wedel
Julian, CA

[Hometown] Crest, CA; [DOB] July 8, 1959; [Ed] Granite Hills High School; [Occ] medical transcriptionist, twenty years; [Hobbies] reading, writing, singing, nature walks; [GA] my sons

The Lord inspired me to write "Heavenly Things" in 1999 on the first anniversary of my father's death. The poem contains many references to verses in the Holy Bible, which records what happens to us after we die. The assurance that Dad finally trusted Christ and his spirit dwells with Him in Heaven comforts me when I'm missing him. I look forward to talking with Dad again someday beside the crystal river after all things are made new (Revelation 21–22). For now, I pray to and trust in "the God of all comfort" (II Corinthians 1:3).

Red Rocker

Slick chrome seats, vinyl cushioned in black,
line the airport's waiting room at Gate B
the black and gray carpet and wide space
between rows inviting momentary rest
from the anxious hustle of passengers
trailing wheeled luggage
to and from their flights.
How surprising to see
at the end of one chrome row,
a solitary wooden rocker, painted red
with slatted seat
facing the large, floor-to-ceiling window,
as if watching the busy tarmac below.
How did that rocker get there?
Who would have thought to make such
a dazzling statement,
a symbol of leisure and relaxation
in a world of speed and destination?
It could only have been a poet,
speaking without words
of the sphere's newest dance,
swirling in and out of the coveted past
like a Sufi meditation
on the value of taking time to listen
to every sojourner's anxious heart
and its seesawing secrets.

Robert Skeele
LaConner, WA

After thirty-four years working among parishioners in Minnesota and college students in Maryland, New Mexico and Vermont, Bob and his wife moved to LaConner, WA in 1987—quite happy to settle down in one place. Following part-time stints at a local boatyard, as a baker and as a facilities manager at a nearby museum, Bob retired to care for his ailing wife. Since her death, he has begun, at eighty-six years of age, to determine his next step, which will probably include living in LaConner most of the time, trying to maintain his old house and, most importantly, trying to write.

Mesmerized

One morning, we sat down together to eat breakfast.
I opened my strawberry Pop-Tart and apple juice,
Glanced up, and saw you staring at me.
You had a smile upon your face.
Our eyes locked:
No words were spoken,
None were needed.
We were mesmerized.
We learned so much in that short amount of time.
Our breakfast remained untouched—
Yet, we were completely satisfied.

Novella Bowling
Corbin, KY

[Hometown] Corbin, KY; [DOB] February 29, 1964; [Ed] MA and Rank 1 in education; [Occ] retired high school teacher; [Hobbies] reading, writing, gardening, horseriding; [GA] surviving two battles with cancer

I am a retired high school English teacher, and I live on a small family farm with my husband Roger and my two daughters, Tiffany and Courtney. Writing is the therapeutic way I express my thoughts and feelings. In each of my poems, I bare my heart and soul, which helps me deal with the obstacles I face each day. As an aspiring poet, I hope my poems can help my readers too. This poem is my first attempt to recapture one of life's most precious, purest moments of innocent love.

A Soldier's Request

As I leave America, the land I love so much,
to go across the sea to toil in foreign soil.
I go abroad to fight aggression and terrorism for peace.

If I am fortunate enough to somehow return to America,
I hope to see again Old Glory waving in the gentle breeze.

If God chooses me not to return home to America,
then I hope to someday meet you at Heaven's gates.

God Bless America

Jim Fields
Miami, OK

[Hometown] Miami, OK; [DOB] March 8, 1944; [Ed] high school; [Occ] retired; [Hobbies] working with youth; [GA] saving a woman's life

My Whole Life

My life began like a knitted blanket with loops connected,
The design continues to create me by circumstances I don't foresee.
Some loops are strong and go on and on,
Some are weak, with snags I don't want to keep,
But keep them I must, they are in the design,
That is part of me and what is mine.
My blanket is not finished, it's full of grief and not complete.
Sometimes the loops unravel, sending me for a spin,
I try hard to fix the direction they are in.
Then there are the loops that go array,
I must bring them back to stay.
My life is in front of me, my future is at stake,
With years of many joys and tears, my blanket's taking shape.
I was a child, a woman , a bride, mother and grandmother.
I see the good and bad, the happy and the sad,
All the memories I have, that created me.
My blanket's almost finished now,
The mistakes I made are hard to see,
It gives me comfort and warmth, but no more strife,
And I will cherish my blanket my whole life.

Christa Melnyczenko
Gaylord, MI

[Hometown] Detroit, MI; [DOB] April 25, 1945; [Ed] two year college; [Occ] real estate agent—sales person; [Hobbies] decoration, writing, and photography; [GA] owning a catering business

I was born in Austria at the end of WWII. My family immigrated to America in 1950. I was the eldest of six children. There were many trials and tribulations in my life. I am now retired and enjoy a more relaxed life with my four children and eleven grandchildren. My husband Mike and I are looking forward to a long and healthy retirement. Writing is in my soul.

The Fifties

The fifties were a grand time when mothers
dressed their girls in full-skirted dresses
to resemble the cute look of a porcelain doll
twirling the hula hoop in rhyme.
No one latched their doors and kids camped
out on the cool wet grass in sleeping bags
to marvel if man would land on Mars.
Noble actor John Wayne was the hero of the day,
as he saddled his horse and galloped away
in the harsh rain with holster in hand
to guide a cowboy to become a gallant man.
Music talent Pat Boone honored women
in songs readily mastered so dear.
And women revered the men without fear.
The movies had a moral message to praise
the sanctity of father, mother, country, and home.
The economy was robust so a kid masked
not his face to endless roam.
Each family had a purpose to express joy
when the song "Happy Trails" was being telecast
as a package gift wrapped in ribbons of hope
for each curious and imaginative boy
who would one precise day be dispatched
to fight in the jungle of the Vietnam War.

Donna Herman
Fairfield, CA

[Hometown] Wheeling, WV; [DOB] November 11, 1954; [Ed] Solano Community College and Writers Digest School; [Occ] Trained Geriatric Aid; [Hobbies] Scrabble; [GA] to pose for a painting that was once placed in the Phoenix Art Museum

I was reading on the web the lyrics to the song "Happy Trails" sung by Roy Rogers and Dale Evans, which gave me the inspiration to write this poem. My writing instructor and published author Arline Chase once stated to me and I quote, "Images in a poem are money in the bank." Her talented insight helped me to become a better writer. I dedicate my poem "The Fifties" to America's children.

Gone

From the hills in
shadows deep,
comes the dead
to mourn and weep.

Gone the sun
for days on end
Gone the warmth
in shared romance

On to truth and life
worthwhile
on to life for
the meek and mild.

Dolores Schilbe
Cadillac, MI

[Hometown] Alpena, MI; [DOB] January 2, 1937; [Ed] BSN in nursing; [Occ] retired—nursing; [Hobbies] knitting and essay writing (and hopefully a book); [GA] raising four children

I am a retired nurse with a BSN from Ferris State University in Big Rapids, MI. When I took English classes for my nursing degree, I found I enjoyed writing and putting a story together. When a local writers group presented a speaker for aspiring writers, I attended and was invited to their meetings. This poem was inspired by a series of personal losses to me—my beautiful yellow Labrador, my only sister, and a close friend. I have found solace in writing this poem. Somehow it made me feel better.

Meandering

Hot and dry,
the caravan
slowly meandered
through dunes
and sage.

Water, a concern...
Nothing crucial yet,
but one couldn't
be too careful.

Thirst has a way
of turning
the mind to
inane things, and then—
it could be too late.

You simply lie down
and hope your
family finds you
and affords
a decent burial.

"Billy!
Get out of that sand
and help your brother
with the lawn...
And no more Kool-Aid
till lunch!"

Dellis Swartzendruber
Monticello, IA

[Hometown] Kalona, IA; [DOB] August 9, 1951; [Ed] BA from the University of Iowa; [Occ] corrections; [Hobbies] painting, sculpture, poetry; [GA] being married to the same woman for thirty-eight years and counting

After playing alone as a small child, my sandbox and buckets of toys offered up faraway worlds only I could imagine..."Meandering" peaks into the world of a child lost in his imagination only to be rudely interrupted by a mother whose patience is being tried when there is work to be done. Oh, to be a child again on a hot, summer afternoon with no worries or fears, letting his or her mind wander to lands unknown, to those safe and wonderful places where only a child can go!

When Head Trumps Heart

The first thing he remembered about Anne
Was her skinny sunburned legs. She was
Fourteen, he was sixteen. Her friend's aunt
Had a cottage on the river. And because
Of forty miles between them they dated once
For dinner when he was eighteen.
To avoid the draft he joined the Navy.
Anne loved his letters. They wrote frequently,
When he was two thousand miles distant.
His first leave was more than a year away.
She urged "going steady," but he saw it unwise
While they were apart for three more years.
He thought the tone of her letters had changed
Before he rode Greyhound home for Christmas.
After supper at Anne's house they washed the dishes.
She told him she'd been seeing an Air Force
Cadet. "Faint heart never won Fair Maiden"
Was not in his vocabulary then
And he donned his coat to leave her when
She said, "Aren't you going to kiss me good-bye?"
"No, Anne, and I wish you well with Air Force guy."
And months later in the Caribbean
Her letters dropped into phosphorescent
Glowing plankton and reflected stars
Of the ship's wake and his head told his heart
"You *might* get over her now, get a grip." Yeah, right.

Friedrich H. Wurzbach
Palmyra, WI

[Hometown] Palmyra, WI; [DOB] November 4, 1941; [Ed] high school, US Navy, two years college; [Occ] bricklayer, artist, school bus driver; [Hobbies] reading, writing, walking, and drawing/painting; [GA] CETA Project Mural, sober twenty-eight years

I was an underachiever in school. After high school, I worked as a dishwasher, landscape laborer, factory worker and then joined the Navy. I attended a twenty-week pattern makers school in 1961. In 1964, I was discharged from the Navy and began working for a tree service. Then, I worked for a well driller, construction worker, salesman, fence-builder, forest service tree planter and bricklayer until 1973. I have two years of college as an art major under my belt; however, I experienced an unsuccessful career and hard time through the '80s and ended up driving a school bus in 1985. Through it all, I read voraciously and wrote letters, stories and poems. My gauche and stupidity regarding women and subsequent regret inspired this poem.

Secret Singer

Into the sunlit woods she'd go,
Running in bare feet.
She didn't want a soul to know.

Early in the morning she would tiptoe,
And then leave the house in fleet.
Into the sunlit woods she'd go.

Her only friend was her shadow,
She kept her gift discreet.
She didn't want a soul to know.

The trees muffled her echo,
So this was her retreat.
Into the sunlit woods she'd go.

Then she'd be sure she's all alone,
And she'd sing a song so sweet.
She didn't want a soul to know.

Sometimes I'd be there also,
Although we never did meet.
Into the sunlit woods she'd go,
She didn't want a soul to know.

Maggie Gray
Shelby, OH

[Hometown] Shelby, OH; [DOB] October 6, 1996; [Ed] current high school student; [Hobbies] art, photography, and writing; [GA] having poetry published

I am a sixteen-year-old high school student. I've always had a love of art and writing. Classes at school and power of the pen have been inspirations. Poetry is a more recent passion I discovered in a creative writing class. This poem is the product of an assignment for the class. It is a fictional idea that was written in a villanelle pattern, which was a fun challenge. My interest in poetry continues to grow, and I love to be inspired. My feet are on the ground, but my head is in the clouds.

Move On

Tears well in the heart, leak from the eyes;
 No one must see, mask the sorrow.
 Emotions in check, move on! move on!
So much loss and pain, what used to be isn't anymore.
Sunshine obscured by clouds and rain.
Precious gifts, taken away, here today gone tomorrow
Not to be seen again, always felt through the pain.
 Tears well in the heart, leak from the eyes;
 No one must see, mask the sorrow.
 Emotions in check, move on! move on!
Cast aside, cast adrift living with doubts.
Wondering why, swimming alone against the tide.
Find a new flow, a safe place to go.
 Tears well in the heart, leak from the eyes;
 No one must see, mask the sorrow.
 Emotions in check, move on move on.
Can't stay in this place too dark, too cold;
Too much sorrow and pain sucking life from me.
 Tears well in the heart, leak from the eyes;
 No one must see, mask the sorrow.
 Emotions in check, move on move on.
Escape the clouds and rain, find sunshine once again.
The past is past, can't go there anymore
Memories will fade and die, no time to cry;
 Mask the sorrow, emotions in check
 Moving on! moving on!

Dale O. McCoy
Denver, CO

[Hometown] *Sterling, CO;* [DOB] *September 26, 1946;* [Ed] *BA University of Northern Colorado, MA Colorado State University;* [Occ] *teacher/ administrator in public education for thirty-seven years;* [Hobbies] *poetry, walking, and lifting weights;* [GA] *my family*

I enjoy observing the many facets of life and then playing with words to try and capture the essence of that which I am observing. My poems cover society, culture, politics, art and relationships. I have written many persona poems, of which this is one. After reading about/watching an interaction between people, I assume the role of one person and try to capture what I believe are the thoughts, feelings and emotions he or she is experiencing.

A Miracle

The unexplainable happening from an unseen source.
The greatest thing that could happen in one's life.
The reaching out and touching of the Master's hand.
Giving aid from nowhere and unexpectedly a miracle happens.
Miracles come from Heaven above,
They come from God that we love.
Sometimes they come on the wings of a dove soaring high in the skies above,
Or reaching down by the touch of His hand.
Reaching out across a barren land.
So pray for a miracle if you are in need.
God will grant you one with His great speed.

Rosemary Toro
Liverpool, NY

[Hometown] Liverpool, NY; [Ed] high school, business school; [Occ] housewife; [Hobbies] writing, art, and gardening; [GA] being a wife, mother and grandmother, being a loving and caring daughter

I am a sixty-eight-year-old and have been writing poems since I was a teenager. A lot of my inspirations come to me in the middle of the night, so I jump up and start writing. I am a mother of four wonderful children and a grandmother of seven. I have a wonderful husband of forty-nine years. I love all kinds of animals, especially dogs. I always had Scotties. I am an artist, and I love to garden. I am a born-again Christian and thank God every day for all He has done in my life.

Unfinished

A sound, a piece, a person; can trigger a memory.
I played a piece, once. It was simple enough.
And linked to that piece is the smell of slide oil,
a major sixth, success, failure,
and success again.
There is a person linked to that piece.
I played the piece at times and hope it brings him back.
But he is gone.
I play the piece over and over again
with precision and perfection. But not with him.
And so, I play it over, and over, and over again.
Because it's not perfect enough.
There's still something to fix.
It's unfinished, just like him.
So maybe, if I play it, it'll trigger memories
And he will come back for a split second.
And maybe, if I do it enough times,
his life will become full, remembered, finished.
But for now, I wait. And try to play perfect.
And I know I'll wait forever, if that's what it takes.
So I'll take a deep breath and close my eyes
And remember.
Remember him forever and always.
Perfection and failure; missed notes and perfect slurs
And we will be happy.
And not unfinished.

Rachel Waterbury
Chagrin Falls, OH

*[Hometown] Chagrin Falls, OH; [DOB] February 8, 1998; [Ed] high school student; [Hobbies] trombone;
[GA] accepted to Cleveland orchestra youth orchestra*

This poem is dedicated to my first trombone teacher, Anthony D. Hopkins.

Click

The chrome covering the knob on the door in the bathroom of our
House is worn through in certain places, revealing the brass
Beneath. To open, the knob must be grasped with the left hand, and

Turned counter-clockwise. The forefinger resting just so,
Between ten o'clock and twelve, while the
Thumb, opposing, rests at two.

An eighth of a turn and click, clash,
The pressure of closing released,
The door opens, chattering as it does.

Outside, when weight is applied, the floor may be silent,
Or it may creak, or in one special place that seems to
Move around, it groans.

For nearly a century after baths have been taken,
Duties done, toilet completed, these sounds have signaled
That something has begun—or ended.

Nearby I hear the sounds, and she comes,
And sits, opposite me, and says,
"There's something I need to tell you."

Mike Welsh
Sioux City, IA

[Hometown] Sioux City, IA; [DOB] February 7, 1946; [Ed] master's in business administration; [Occ] retired; [Hobbies] puppy care; [GA] being a dad

One Step at a Time

Look at you, gal, in such a rush
It's making you out for a lush
Searchin' for applause.
Hell, you can't even pause.
Reachin' for it
Whatever it may be, I see,
Some days that still is me.
Ridin' on elevators gets me down,
I take the steps, it's much more sound.
No waitin' for Godot, it seems
Better on your own steam.
Shakespeare said, "Lovers dead
Who go too fast, won't last;
Better go steady, but slow.

One step at a time, you're gonna make it.
One step at a time, you're gonna take it.
One step at a time, together: you and I.
One step at a time, we're gonna work it.
One step at a time, not gonna shirk it
One step at a time, your dreams are waitin' for you.

Illa C. Howe
Germantown, MD

[Hometown] Washington, D.C.; [DOB] June 18, 1948; [Ed] LAMDA London and NYU for film; [Occ] salesperson, playwright, equity and SAG; [Hobbies] singing; [GA] being a part of NYC Production stage and cable TV

Life

A bother
A strain
A heavy, heavy load.

Why stay?
Who cares?
Love's lost!
And all at my cost.

Great pain.
A broken heart.
Such heartache.
A lonely, lonely life.

Linda A. Avellino
Carrollton, OH

Poetry for me is a great way of expressing how I feel. I have been "expressing myself" since I was seven years old. My father always carried a poem that I wrote for him when I was in the third grade. My grandfather was a published poet in the thirties and forties. I am thankful for the artistic genes I have inherited. I am inspired to write most of the time whether I am happy, sad, etc. I usually have a handful of notes that I have jotted, a verse or two, stuffed in my purse. Most people have grocery lists, I have poems.

You Must Go

Take one step of faith
At a time
As you place your hands
Inside of Mine,
I will lead you
Where you must go—
Just follow the path
That I will show,
Wait upon Me
And listen
For the still small voice
Of my Holy Spirit,
And when I say go—
You must go without hesitation
Or reservation—
For this leap of faith
In front of you
You must take now,
So trust in Me with all your heart
And I will bring you to a place
Where joy is abundant
And love will overflow.

Hannah M. Clayson
Hemlock, NY

[Hometown] Hemlock, NY; [DOB] August 21, 1988; [Ed] Calvary Chapel School of Ministry; [Hobbies] writing poetry/songs, reading, and playing guitar

As I Rise Heavenward!

With my loving family at my side,
Jesus came and met me there.
He took my hand saying, "Come with Me,
Their wounded hearts I will repair."

As we rise, I look at you all,
My family crying over me!
Seeing your love for each other
Makes me proud as I can be!

My body now being healed,
We rise to Heaven above.
Jesus holding me in His arms,
I can feel His compassion and love!

Oh what a wonderful place!
I have family here too!
As they welcome me with open arms,
We will be here to welcome you!

Neal A. Carl
Endwell, NY

I started out to write a poem the day after my father-in-law passed away. This poem came to me as if my father-in-law were speaking it into my ears! I typed on my computer as these words came and when I was done I was overwhelmed at the message, the vision and how it appeared to come to me! I know there are others who have been in the same situation. Many times God will give us little blessings and I believe He allowed me to hear my father-in-law one last time! God is Good all the time!

The Bucket List

As I approach the ripe young age of sixty plus
Additions to my bucket list have increased a lot.
During the year I checked off two without much fuss
This unusual incident has formed many other thoughts.

The first hit was in February, the greatest of all feats,
Our beautiful granddaughter was born for all to cheer.
She smiled and cooed and my heart skipped some beats,
Great emotion and joy of new life shed with a tear.

Paige is now five months old and her playful nature shows
Her "sweet pink cheeks" reflect the love from all around.
Those bright blue eyes sparkle as she grabs her small toes
This child has created an awareness not easily found.

In June a very big class reunion took place on a ship
Some classmates were aboard waiting to meet face to face.
We partied, toured, met for dinner all part of a great trip
This noted event was memorable giving each their own space.

This dreaded bucket list caused many ideas to ponder
Bringing a sense that time is quickly fleeting away.
But as you write down your list of special wonders
Eagerness emerges while planning those rare days.

It is time to think about the rest of our lives on earth
What you want to accomplish, see, do, or give back.
We have all satisfied many desires since our birth
Imagine those rewarding acts to help stay on track.

A wise person once stated to me in secret
"Live life to the fullest and don't leave with regrets."

Carole Ortale-Curtis
Rancho Palos Verdes, CA

[Hometown] Rancho Palos Verdes, CA; [DOB] August 15; [Ed] BA degree and certification in career counselling, coach; [Occ] career counselor and coach; [Hobbies] writing poetry, travel, and photography; [GA] to write and publish a poetry book

I have recently lost several friends and family members, and it made me think about all the things that they wanted to accomplish while on this earth and did not get the chance to complete. Then I realized I should consider writing a list and start the process of finishing some of my accomplishments, like traveling and giving back to the community. I have begun working on this and was very surprised that I had already achieved two of the points this year. I am also working on getting my book of poems published in the near future.

The Two Dead Women

One day in the middle of the night,
two dead women got into a fight.
They drew their fingers, and shot each other.
A dead police man heard the noise,
and shot those two dead women who were fighting in the middle of the night.
If you don't believe this lie is true,
just ask the blind lady, she saw everything, she will tell you the truth.

Detra Wilson
Charlston, IL

[Hometown] Charleston, IL; [DOB] July 26, 1977; [ED] twelfth grade; [Hobbies] music, writing poems;
[GA] getting a poem published

A Brother's Bond

You didn't know my struggle
But recognized the pain
Kept hope alive
Believed in my dream
Ups and downs
May take a wrong turn
That's what life's about
Lessons learned
Taught me everything
Pick myself up
Every time I fall
Showed me how to be a man
Taught me to stand tall
You never left
When I felt abandoned
You're my brother
Reason I'm still standing

Christian Rayl
Ankeny, IA

*[Hometown] Des Moines, IA; [DOB] March 14, 1993; [Ed] AA in business; [Occ] construction; [Hobbies]
I enjoy basketball and writing lyrics; [GA] graduating high school after struggling my first two years*

*There was a time when I felt alone and my brother taught me how to stand on my own. This is my way of
thanking him. Jorge this is for you.*

The Mighty Cross

Long ago there lived a mighty majestic saguaro cactus
Basking in the Arizona desert, his arms reaching toward the sky.
After years of standing tall and proud
It fell to the desert ground and slowly died.

The flesh on the saguaro cactus frame
Rotted and left only the ribs to remain.
A man walking by picked up the wood from the pile
And carved out of it a beautiful cross for his child.

He looked at his child and explained with great pride
It was completely for us that our Savior died
His heart would not sway as He was nailed to the cross
That we may be saved and our souls never lost.

With a hug and a smile he told his child
We must never forget who we really are
Always keep Jesus tucked deep in our hearts
Spread the word of His love near and far.

Jesus too was a proud and mighty man
Who loved us more than Himself
And after all the time that has passed
Even today His love is still felt.

When you look upon this rugged cross
As you give thanks to Jesus and pray
What once was mighty in all its splendor
Is still a powerful symbol to this day.

Madelin Vaugn Flannery
Peoria, AZ

[Hometown] Peoria, AZ; [DOB] May 21, 1943; [Ed] some college, nursing, real estate; [Occ] many different hats, a lot of owned business; [Hobbies] poetry; [GA] loving my kids with much joy

My poetry usually tells a story, has a moral, or is written with humor. Good, bad, or a hard lesson, I appreciated all that life gave me. Though married four times, I had to support my children and started many businesses. My poetry got shoved in a box for the future. I wrote this poem fifteen years ago to go along with "Cactus Crosses" from the Sonoran dessert saguaro that we made and sold. All my teachers in school predicted I would be a writer. I must sort through hundreds of poems and put them in a book for publication.

Pink Collar Workers

There's waxers and wavers
And carrot cake bakers,
Telephone talkers
And high-wire walkers.
There's tip-toey dancers
And teachers with answers,
Balance-bar beamers
And tree hug extremers.
There are stiletto-bound hookers
And cat-walking lookers.
Flu shot injectors
And assembly inspectors.
Even age will proclaim
That some jobs will remain
Like churchy bell chimers and
Parody rhymers.

Kristi Herring
Sun City West, AZ

I grew up in a small town in Kansas, loving the wonderful and humorous works of cartoonist Walt Kelly's "Pogo." Now I'm retired, and living in Sun City West, AZ. I've enjoyed pressing the pencil now and then writing poetry, with several poems published in anthology books. I'm also a watercolor artist, along with writing poetry. I've illustrated seven books and two were my own: Marty's Barage Band, *a children's book, and* Through Artist's Eyes, *a book of poetry with some of my paintings attached. The most fun I've had with poetry was the open mike reading in front of an audience, at the "Cowboy Poet Gathering" in Prescott, AZ. One day I was wondering why they always talked about "Blue Collar Workers" a job title for working men but nothing for women? Well, here's a poem I wrote for women, "Pink Collar Workers."*

Muses in the Making

In a choir of Heaven's reach,
there is a muse to be lovingly found,
a great talent to be beseeched,
a melody of magnificent sound!
I hear the thoughts on scroll and parchment,
with admiration do honorably follow,
God's intense imagination,
being placed, humbled, praised, exalted, and even,
immortally sent!
The tears, the smiles, the blood, the heart, and soul,
is on a constant battle,
a never-ending run.
It sparkles, it dulls, it laughs, and it cries, it quotes and sings,
most marvelous things.
Hear the newest muses ring!
Humans, souls, angels, demons,
all forced to witness, recognize
Heaven's never truly done.
They must follow the path… of a great story,
of love, loss, comedy, justice, or vengeance's wrath.
We all find, follow,
and record the whole infinite universe's sorrow!
Listen, write, sing, and say,
for there is always a beautiful glorious ballet, play.
A muse is always in the making,
as there are always tragically hearts breaking

Sherry Wilbur
Wichita, KS

[Hometown] Wichita, KS; [DOB] April 21, 1975; [Ed] Alamose High, Conway Community College, Las Vegas, NV; [Occ] housewife, mom, writer; [Hobbies] reading, writing, gardening, and listening to music; [GA] my two kids

Music, art, and literature pretty much inspired this, along with life, nature, romance, and pain. You cannot live numbly and truly live. I believe that everything happens for a reason and the most beautiful things come from our pains.

Future World

Higher technology
Will take over
With telescopes capable of studying
A supernova.

Electromagnetic
Waves
And radio frequencies
Are the science of the day.

Interdimensional
Gateways
Invisible vortex
Is where our path lays.

Vast clouds of gas
Into the realms of comprehension sight.
Unlike the past
Sunlight that illuminates into the night.

Supernatural circumstance
Manifestation of the mind.
Not to those who have the knowledge
To understand this great find.

Life as we know it
Is nonexistent.
Bit by bit
It faded away.

Margaret Worley
Watertown, TN

[Hometown] Watertown, TN; [DOB] February 2, 1960; [Ed] grade school, sales representative; [Occ] salesperson; [Hobbies] reading, poetry, science, and cooking; [GA] published work

I am a fan of science. I was inspired to write a poem about how the world was changing and what might be in our near future. Technology seems to be happening so fast that the world can't seem to catch up with it. More planets and star systems are being found every day. It's a whole new world out there just to be discovered. So, I encourage everyone to search out God's great wonders. I thank Eber & Wein Publishing for giving me the chance to express my mind on this subject. Thanks to everyone who encouraged me to write.

Power

I am the fighter, I am your freedom
I am your fate, I am who I choose to be
I will not roam the streets.
Careless intentions, lay for the night
Fire inside, you burn—I die
Fight knight, knife or dagger?
Sheath the beggar, murder is deal
Kneel and pray, hope for the day
When freedom is free
And blood not pay
I am the ghost, I am your guilt
I am your ambition, I am what mask I wear
And will tear from your chest
The blackest void
Toy with your mind, leave it behind
Crumble the dust beneath
Sheath the emotion, make an act an action
Beg for the beggar's breath
Whisper warrants of death
I make not the wish, I make not the thought
I make not the puppet strings
That bind and demand
I make the command.

Hannah Brace
Wetaskiwin, AB Canada

[Hometown] Wetaskiwin, AB; [DOB] February 7, 1995; [Ed] high school diploma; [Occ] cook at Smitty's Restaurant; [Hobbies] photography, music; [GA] graduated high school

Lullaby

Please sing me, sweet,
cultivating soothing song.
Engraved, de-vouted, high pitched,
and calm, full of dreamy and
drowsy words, the doves above
overheard. Lay my head upon
your breast; as you sing a
lullaby, to put me to rest.

Stanley E. James II
Long Beach, CA

[Hometown] North Long Beach, CA; [DOB] January 10, 1990; [Ed] Wilson High School; [Occ] urban poet; [Hobbies] reading/writing; [GA] graduating high school

Chagrin

Oh, ancient mystery
Waves crashing onto shore
Oh mystical thoughts
Over and over again once more
Chimes of life
Ringing throughout time
Bringing forth emotions
Affecting us with rhyme
Why are we moving
Towards the end of time
Listen to the voices way
Above the crowds
Strive to reach beyond the
Highest cumulus clouds
Keep in touch deep within
And realize your own chagrin

Poet Goldberg
Pompano Beach, FL

My poetry comes from experience and my innermost self, affected by people, places and things. Poetic verse enables one to express one's feelings, philosophies and views related to a given subject. "Chagrin" was written from an experience dealing with residents living at a nursing home who affected my life. Dealing with the public on a grand scale over the years has enabled me to understand myself better and to count my blessings. Many others are not as fortunate and become forgotten. Doing for others, using compassion and humor is what it's all about. Carpe Diem does apply!

Diamonds in the Night

Spellbound, I looked up to see a sparkling sight
suspended by invisible threads
under a balmy moonlit night.
Alive like flames as it gently sways in the evening breeze,
making brilliant roadways of celestial delight
peeking through a translucent bowl,
and as I gaze in wonder
it moves me to my very soul.
Dripping like a delicate water fountain of light,
weighed down with jewel-like diamonds in the night.
Whoever has created this glorious thing
has the artistic ability to make one's heart sing.
As I sit and ponder,
a movement captures the corner of my eye—
glancing over I see the creator of this masterpiece
sailing down on a ribbon from a spot up high.
He takes his place in the center of his home,
a tiny yellow spider, framed in the twinkling filmy beauty
… that's his alone.

Patricia LeCompte
Ottawa, ON Canada

[Hometown] Ottawa, Ontario; [DOB] April 16, 1933; [Ed] grade eight; [Occ] mother and housewife; [Hobbies] short stories, poetry, swimming; [GA] my five children

I have lived in Ottawa for eighty years. I've always liked to write essays and poetry. Of my five children, three are quite artistic, especially in photography. One daughter Dyana sends me pictures of creatures she captures in her garden (butterflies, bumblebees, spiders, etc.), and I write poems about them. My other daughter Darlene picks a word for me to compose a poem around. So, my poetry is about specific things in creation that are uniquely beautiful. This particular poem is from a picture of a magnificent spiderweb that was accidentally hit with water when my daughter was hosing off the porch. I am always surprised when someone in the publishing business tells me my humble efforts are indeed worth the read.

Change of Seasons

Summer arrived late and went fast,
The summer solstice is now long past.
There's a hint of autumn in the air—
Frosty lawns, mornings crisp and fair.

The orange glow of pumpkins in the fields,
And high above...a lazy hawk wheels.
Where corn once stood, the rows are bare;
Migrating birds now forage there.

Mother Nature paints portraits of the trees
With her palette of multi-colored leaves,
Inspiring artists and photographers to capture
The beauty of the scenes they enrapture.

Rising full and yellow in the East,
A brilliant harvest moon is a feat
For the eyes on a late September night,
Bathing the land in its silvery light.

But like the moon, the time of seasons wane,
Each surrendering to the next, the cycle to sustain.
And man, like the seasons of song and rhyme,
Waxes and wanes with the sands of time.

Leslie L. Newton Jr.
Cape Elizabeth, ME

[Hometown] Cape Elizabeth, ME; [DOB] August 19, 29; [Ed] general education with two years of college; [Occ] retired safety engineer; [Hobbies] poetry and golf; [GA] marrying my wife of sixty-three years

I am eighty-four years old, and my wife and I have been married for sixty-three great years. I served in the U.S. Air Force during the Korean War years. I have written hundreds of poems beginning with those I wrote to my wife during those years. I have self-published several books of my poetry, principally for family and friends. Also, many of my poems have been published by Eber & Wein Publishing, the International Library of Poetry and other local periodicals. Inspiration for my poems emanates from personal experiences, memories, and current and historical events. I hope I have many years yet in which to share my poetic gift with others.

Stepping Stones

Stepping stones underneath my feet,
Where fierce lilies force and fight their way through.
Days past laid behind, today below, tomorrow just ahead
All a memory of something done, of something new.
Sometimes I trip and lose my place,
But the stepping stones are sure to direct me back
This is my life, my life's race,
Not here on its own, but each carefully laid,
Not by human hands or a coincidental accident.
I can't see the end, but my Builder knows,
For by Him it was long ago made.
He walks by my side day and night,
Directing and guiding me when the sun goes down
He holds my hand and leads me in the light,
He'll never leave my side, and I the same.

Lara Fraser
Shelburne County, NS Canada

[Hometown] Clyde River, NS; [DOB] February 24, 1997; [Occ] camp counselor; [Hobbies] writing and horseback riding; [GA] having poems published

I'm a sixteen-year-old girl who has a passion for writing. When I write my poetry, it comes from the heart; it is not something that can be forced, as it comes naturally. And ever since Jesus came in to my life, it seems He's all I can write about. I hope you enjoy!

Seeds in My Garden

My inner garden is lush, beautiful and serene—my private retreat to relax and unwind, a labor of love—my emotional lifeline. Seeds lovingly planted by women who nurtured and molded the inner me, provide a rainbow of colors and beauty that anchor my path of destiny...

A profusion of blooming flowers, plants and hardy shrubs—spread as far as the eye can see—grow from seeds of courage, integrity and humility. A carpet of rose petals befitting royalty, grown from seeds of compassion, empathy and affinity, are a poignant reminder that those who are in need also have the right to hopes, dreams, and dignity.

Gigantic lily pads bob and weave with pugnacious brawn, dancing a jig on turbulent waters, while providing me safe passage through life's perilous storms. A bounty of fibrous vines that anchor my climb up life's steepest hills, grow from seeds of tenacity, resolve, and strength of will. Exotic gardenias wearing a cloak of heady perfume emit a jolt of electrifying passion that launches me over the moon...

When the burdens of life begin to take a toll, I retreat to my inner garden to nurture my soul—and commune with the women who welcomed me into the fold.

These are the seeds in my garden.

Beverley E. Johnson
Boston, MA

[Hometown] Boston, MA; [DOB] May 16, 1953; [Ed] college graduate; [Occ] real estate consultant; [Hobbies] writing, gardening, reading; [GA] writing poetry

This poem was inspired by the love and nurturing received from the women in my family.

A Nurse's Call

We all have a call to life's open door,
The instant we are born—
We leave that inner solitude
Of womb, and enter life night or morn.
We grow in love and wisdom true
Through infancy and adulthood anew.
With His love in our heart
His strength to the weak do we impart
Inspired are we at the infant's first cry,
Awed are we at man's last sigh.

Artists portray life on canvas white
We embrace his image day and night.
We stroke away the malignant blue
And paint the picture all anew.
Mental, physical, spiritual all three
Our instruments to aid mortality
We as nurses must fulfill our call
For God has appointed us, one and all.
This special gift of life to guard
With purest love through labor hard.
This our path on Earth to tread
To vision Christ by each sick bed. God holds our candle to light our way
Even through the darkest day
Then when we are old, to always rejoice
That we were nurses by His choice

Dolly Bradt
Amherstburg, ON Canada

[Hometown] Amherstburg, ON; [DOB] October 31, 1938; [Ed] registered nurse; [Occ] registered nurse (retired); [Hobbies] reading, poetry, knitting, and gardening; [GA] family love and Eber & Wein's recognition of my poems

I wrote "A Nurse's Call" in 1959 (age nineteen) for graduation from nurse's training (original thirty-eight lines—reduced to twenty-six lines) and submitted by request of family and friends now—fifty-four years later. Today I am a seventy-four-year-young retired registered nurse (fifty years practice) and a widow seventeen years (married forty years). I am a mother (one son), grandmother (three grandsons—seventeen, fourteen, twelve years), and have two sisters. My inspiration for poetry is a gift from God and He guides me to put words on paper. Love from one's soul to another—to provide comfort, solace, empathy, compassion, understanding, and peace.

Mortal Flight

From day to day and month to month,
They change before our eyes.
The time goes fleeting softly by,
Filled with memories that will not die.

A small, wee hand soiled from play,
Laying lifeless with sleep;
Dirty face content to rest,
Energy spent they could not keep.

As the days go marching past,
They grow so fond and dear.
We cannot stand for them to leave,
Although the time grows near.

So they go into the world
To make their way alone.
Now we wonder how they are
And wish they were home.

Wayne Firestone
Dubuque, IA

[Hometown] Dubuque, IA; [DOB] September 17, 1927; [Ed] two years of college; [Occ] retired; [Hobbies] writing; [GA] living

When I was sixteen (1943), I was a merchant SRA man on a troop transport in the South Pacific. Subsequently, at eighteen, I was a soldier in the occupation of Japan. When I returned home, I went to college for two years, worked for the government twenty years in various capacities and ended in the position of production controller and budget analyst. Becoming disenchanted with the daily monotonous routine of the job, I quit and became a greyhound kennel owner and worked at that for another thirty-nine years. This information has nothing to do with poetry but does give an indication of my disparate nomadic life.

Life, Life...

Life carries struggle, pain and has its mistakes of the day.
Life is not to cause pain, sadness, bitterness
Or to cause broken hearts.
We cannot fix or erase pain of words of others.
In life we do have a choice to forgive and forget.
Life gives us pain, tears and makes us
Fight for our life. Life is not easy.
Behind every tear is a performance for today,
And for tomorrow's strength and hope.
Life is beautiful, when it comes with gift of
Happiness, joy and health, to have this gift you have everything.
We should only worry about today and tomorrow.
Every day life is an experience for tomorrow.
At end of day, we ask ourselves what it will cost
To bring back yesterday's day...
No power or money brings back a day of yesterday.
We are here to live life, do the best, stand with no fear.
Be thankful for life, thank God for every day's blessing.
Take every day with smiles in clouds,
That will raise happiness in our hearts.
Life is valuable, cherish the moments.
Life is all memories to hold in our hearts forever.
Life is beautiful, always shine like a star.
Live life to the fullest. Live here, live now.

Renate Ursula Aksoy
Mississauga, ON Canada

First I say thank You, God, for every day's blessing. Thank You, God, for life. Thank you to my mom, to my amazing sisters Christina and Leila, and my baby sister Majvor, who are always there for me. Thank you to the rest of my family—my brothers-in-law, nephews, and beautiful niece Emily. Always love you all.

A Paradox in Paradise

I listen to the murmur of the air's breath
deep in the ancient forest,
A welcomed visitor in a summer sanctuary.

In the cool, the damp.
The moisture clings to and cools the skin.
The wind passes. I am almost cold in the summer heat.

I leave the path and wander in this harmony.
Where heat and cool, moist and dry, shade and light,
Make my senses come to life.

Jo-Anne Maree Pigram
Constitution Hill, NSW Australia

[Hometown] Parramatta, Sydney, New South Wales, Australia; [DOB] September 1, 1983; [Ed] some college; [Hobbies] poetry, yoga, pilates, bushwalking; [GA] being selected for this publication

All my life, I have wanted to become a recognized poet. I began writing at a young age and have always been encouraged to continue writing. Thank you for another opportunity to share my work with the world. In this poem, I escape reality in an ancient forest where a world full of competing dualities come together to ironically create a surreal paradise of harmony where I bask, full of love.

Moonlight

Shimmering turmoil of the silvery waves
As they ripple, swish and continuously sway
Often upon a rock they beat
The forceful waters, delightfully spray.
And of a night this glory's told
When Moon does shine so bright
The yellow beams, the waters meet
And beauty is behold in sight.
For lovers this enchantment holds
Something precious to their hearts
For time does pass, but ne'er the sight
For it has long before been told
So if you should rove to the sea one night
To pass the time away
Keep it dear this immortal sight
For it is there in you to stay.

Colleen N. Frankland
Kariong, NSW Australia

[Hometown] Sydney, Australia; [DOB] June 4, 1947; [Ed] teaching degree; [Occ] teacher; [Hobbies] art, literature, craft; [GA] poetry published

I have written poetry from an early age. I was mostly inspired by the works of Wordsworth, Robert Herrick and all the old English poets. "Moonlight" comes from the beauty surrounding all the beaches and inlets around the coast of Australia. Many of my poems have been published in the International Poetry Society books throughout the years. I have traveled the world, and all the knowledge I have received is imprinted on me forever.

Protected

I built walls around myself
   invisible walls
   strong walls
   protective walls
hung with calendars and to-do lists
activities and commitments

My walls have doors and windows
   locked doors
   narrow windows
   of leaded glass
I wear the keys to my locks and knobs
on a fine chain hung from my heart

Within my walls, behind locked doors
   I built my nest
   I built my life
   I rebuilt myself
removing masks, I hid old facades away
and faced myself by myself

And then slip'd into the world
   into starlight
   into chaos
   into magic
leaving my door unlocked and window open
calendar pages floating away.

Kim H. Sherman
Eugene, OR

One More Chance

Beyond the veil! Where mortals
Would never dare to stand.
Fleet mysterious moments
Upon the Golden Strand
Swift uncharted journey
Past boundless galaxy
Into undreamt dimensions
Into eternity!
Faded now the luster
Of treasures left behind
While all life's panorama
Plays instant in our mind.
But God, who knows our weakness
Who made our feet of clay
Has patiently consented
To grant us one more day.
A day to love our brother,
Embrace sun, rain, and sod
To tune our very heartbeat
Unto the heart of God
To cherish each awakening
To laugh, to sing, to dance!
And thankful every moment
He gives us one more chance.

John E. Dunne
Seminole, FL

[Hometown] Waterpiet, NY; [DOB] May 18, 1919; [Ed] high school graduate; [Occ] retired from Veterans Administration 1976; [Hobbies] golf, piano, vocal, and poetry; [GA] made five holes in one

Some years ago a friend had a life-after-death experience, inspiring my poem "One More Chance." I met my bride when she was fifteen and I was twenty. August 12, 2013 will be our seventy-first wedding anniversary. We have four children, ten grandchildren, and twenty-seven greats. I retired in 1976 from the Veterans Administration. A veteran of WWII, I served in Europe. I compose songs and sing them in church, accompanying myself on the piano. God has been good!

The World Is Still Not Safe for Kids

The world is still not safe for kids
abuse of children who are within the home
The killing of kids moved from home to schools
Newtown is a good example of this.

This brought about the gun laws
and then there came the abortion law
To help stop the killing of kids
This is to try and keep our kids safe.

The world is not thinking of the kids
The world is thinking of keeping their guns
How would they have peace of mind
And not to depend on drug abuse alone?

Where they can get high on drugs
How can they find guns to kill and rob
Without guns and drugs, their lives are empty
The world for some people has gone insane.

Rudolph Ramsey Jr.
San Antonio, TX

*[Hometown] San Antonio, TX; [DOB] November 23, 1942; [Ed] high school, military; [Occ] food service;
[Hobbies] playing drums, art; [GA] military retirement after twenty-six years of service*

Mirrors of Judgment

My truths have been unfolding
Since the day I was born
I am not brilliant, I am not beauty
I am a child in others' eyes
Or I am a freak to the onlookers.

Mirrors are my form of judgment
People do not see the real me
Only the me they wish to mold into something...perfect
I wish to cry I wish to scream
But I cannot bring myself to do it.

I break away the glass one piece at a time
There before me is a scene
A scene where it is just I
The sea, the trees and sunset all aglow
No one around to judge, no one to tell me different
No mirrors of judgment...
Tears gently fall from my eyes
Onto the smooth bed of sand
There I lay on the warm beach
Content with my life, content with myself
Content with a scene of beauty.

Tara-Lynn Courtepatte
Edmonton, AB Canada

[Hometown] Edmonton, AB; [DOB] June 24, 1992; [Ed] collegiate studies for digital graphics and communications; [Occ] print industry; [Hobbies] writing; [GA] being published

I began writing in junior high school when my uncle told me, "You have a gift to feel what someone else is feeling and take that feeling and put it into words for them." That never left me, which led me to write until I would have writer's block for days because I used every bit of words and inspiration I had. Nowadays my pen or pencil still moves freely over the paper, but my poems have become more in depth and my ideas have made people or loved ones cry silent tears, which I have taken to heart to know that my gift to write would never leave me. Writing has become a part of my life, and I do not think I could live without writing. It is my life.

In the Mirror

I look in the mirror; I do not like the person I see.
Why couldn't I look the way I wanted to be?
An energetic, ambitious person with a smile
I was always willing to go the extra mile.
Always active and able to work
I had no idea that a disease in my body lurked.
With a butterfly pattern on my face
I could no longer run the race.
With very little energy and joint pain so fierce
My whole body it seemed to pierce.
An autoimmune disease hid for years.
Now tore my life apart and my heart was in tears.
Now. I look in the mirror; I like the person I see.
I am a child of God and I am still me.
Holding my hand, Jesus guides my day.
He knows the obstacles I will meet on my way.
He knows my life plan
With Him, I know I can
Visit valleys and climb the mountain high.
My eye on the cross, I lift my prayers to the sky.
I am not a size two model or able to run and dance
I am blessed by God and still ready to take a chance.
Oh, I look in the mirror; I do like the person I see.
God loves me and walks beside me.

Patricia L. Murphy
Fort Wayne, IN

[Hometown] Fort Wayne, IN; [DOB] December 9, 1938; [Ed] early childhood development certification and business major; [Occ] retired administrative assistant; [Hobbies] writing poetry, scrapbooking, and reading; [GA] a mother, grandmother and great-grandma

Bless Me O Lord

Bless me, oh Lord, you are my king.
To you I will lift my voice and sing.
My heart and soul belong to you,
I hope I show it in all I do.

Bless me, oh Lord, you are my Savior.
With you I have found favor.
Help me witness your love
Like you did when you sent a dove.

Bless me, oh Lord, you are my God.
Let my path be the path you trod.
I know that you are great;
Help me tell others before it's too late.

Bless me, oh Lord, you are my Messiah.
There is no need to deny you.
That is why I shall shout
Your holy name all about.

Kathy Shingleton Jamison
Taylorsville, KY

[Hometown] Taylorsville, KY; [DOB] December 26, 1974; [Ed] high school graduate; [Occ] full-time mom; [Hobbies] reading, writing; [GA] my kids, being a good mom

I am thirty-eight years old and a full-time mother of two children. I am a born again Christian. All my writing talent belongs to Jesus Christ. My kids inspire me a lot, though. I write about things I know about. I am a high school graduate. I write in my spare time, but it's not my whole life. I love to read, go to church and spend time with my kids. Life for me is great. Writing poetry is something I do to share God's work with others and what he has done for me. God bless you all.

My Invitation: And Mona Lisa Smiled

and so it goes, he knows me too well,
in a portrait pose where he came too close;
there's nothing that will compel
an answer to the riddle my smile chose.
I like it well his portrait of me
for the smile that pleads to deceive;
love's victim of the selfish kind
a relief to the trouble in his mind.
the colours scheme around the stains,
for the name of love implores someone to blame,
it's not for his art he chose to remain
but for this desire to catch aflame.
unaware of the means in laying out a life
he holds eagerly to the magicks of his art,
needless is the nature of my heart;
an absent idol to hold him through the night.
no heed taken to who might be around,
concerned only with his need upon my crown,
he lingers on what may pass for a smile
and misses the invitation to stay awhile.
along my frames does lay the fault,
the canvas can never be all that he wants,
ain't it strange how out of his whole life
it's never love that's the real prize.

George Wood
Ottawa, ON Canada

[Hometown] Ottawa, ON; [DOB] November 23, 1978; [Ed] English literature at Ottawa University; [Occ] government and public service; [Hobbies] writing, reading, music, and collecting muses; [GA] winning first place in first poetry contest.

I began my life of poetry at fifteen; it was a way of dealing with all the hormones that raged around my head. I was inspired by Alice Walker's poetry, her portrayal of the outsider and its struggle really connected with me. It wasn't until university that I really understood how amazing the poetic experience could be, on me and those who opened themselves to it. I have always endeavoured to be honest and open in my own poetry, creating a place for the reader to decipher their own meaning, while being true to my own.

The Lord's Eraser

I sat and thought of life's journey
What beauty it shall be if I have the key
To all the successes that life may bring
If only right directions shall I attain.

I took a pencil and started to draw
The paths to take, the lines to make
Frustrations arise, perfection impossible
Why can't I ever make a red ribbon?

I heard a whisper deep in my soul
"My child here's my eraser all
A corner there, an extended line here
They needed trimming, they needed fixing."

I paused and thought and searched my heart
"Yes Lord, color may change, corrections
may hurt. But Lord, you're right
Your eraser is best for red ribbon bright."

Adelfa G. Lorilla
Seagoville, TX

This poem was written when I was thinking of how awesome God is. Things may not look good in our life, but if we look deeper we will see the beauty that God creates. I am married to Ricardo M. Lorilla. We have eight children (Karen, Jan, Zheena, Andrei, Armi, May, Ric and Jesse) and seven grandchildren. I have an MA in English and I am now retired.

Made of Stardust

Look up to the dark of night,
Distant stars sparkling bright.

Come back down and look into each other's eyes:
Starry, dreaming enchanted life spiritually divine.

Mysterious and magical,
Her beautiful ethereal.

Impressions charismatic communication through our dedication.
His heroic times for adventurous perseverance determination.

This uncritical sense of well-being.
Seeing and feeling great in love's welcoming.

Built of quality and success,
We bring peace to this place.

Suns and planets,
Earthly living presence.

From below to above,
Made of stardust.

Robert Tusim
Walkerton, ON Canada

*[Hometown] Walkerton, ON; [DOB] July 20, 1983; [Ed] Sacred Heart High School graduate; [Occ] writer
and author of my first poetry book, I Guardian; [Hobbies] playing guitar and reading books; [GA] becoming
a published poet and uncle*

Prayer for the Grieving Hearts

God hear our prayers. Bring comfort to the hearts that are frequently engulfed with waves of pain, sorrow. Tears often fall freely, falling beyond our lips, obscuring all to us so empty and bereft we feel.

Help us in our darkest hours, when we walk the dark tunnel alone, with no one beside us but our sorrow which closes out all light,

When answers to our question are no longer there, be our light, be our hope and salvation.

Let our grieving hearts find nurture in the companionship of others. Let us find peace, hope, faith in the beauty of Your creation, and time be our healer.

God, You have them in Your keeping, their memories are our keepsake, forever they will be carried in our hearts.

In loving memories our loved ones live in eternal life. Though we do not see them, we feel them, their presence is with us in our keepsake and forevermore.

Diana Tkalec
St. Leonard, QC Canada

[Hometown] Montreal, QC; [DOB] March 8, 1968; [Ed] college diploma creative arts; [Occ] administration; [Hobbies] writing, drawing, reading; [GA] having a poem published

Many people have experienced a loss of a loved one. I too have lost a beloved brother recently in 2010. I know what tragedy can do to a family. This poem was written as a tribute to the families who have lost a loved one in the tragic train wreck of Lac Magantec in Quebec and for the loss of my brother, his memory. Rest in peace.

Why Won't You Ride the Elevator with Me?

Why did you step into the elevator car
behaving like you were a famous star,
only to leave again when you saw it was only me,
someone with whom you blatantly disagreed?
Was it because I was white and you were Hispanic?
Did this difference in our skins make you panic,
or were you were just angry
because our thoughts and beliefs were not in harmony?
Just because we don't agree
doesn't mean that we shouldn't treat each other with respect and humility,
so why won't you ride in the elevator with me?
Why won't you ride in the elevator with me?

Why won't you ride in the elevator with me?
Is this because I was victorious in the election of new secretary
and you were not, and you didn't feel like behaving in the way that you ought,
or was this because I simply disagreed with you at a meeting?
Oh, how respect from others is so fleeting!
So I ask again, why won't you ride in the elevator with me,
even though we don't agree socially or politically?

Barbara Hagen
Palm Desert, CA

[Hometown] *Palm Desert, CA;* [DOB] *June 6, 1964;* [Occ] *writer;* [Hobbies] *bowling, movies, writing;* [GA] *I self-published a poem anthology.*

I was standing in an elevator waiting to go up when a woman with whom I had had a disagreement came up to the elevator shouting, "Hold the elevator, hold the elevator!" When she saw that I was standing alone inside the elevator, the woman passed through the elevator doors, and then she said, "I've changed my mind. I'm going to ride up with my friends!" This poem is dedicated to all those who have been victim of discrimination or prejudice in their lifetimes

The Eagle

I stand and gaze through the smog below
While a gleaming sun makes his feathers glow.
I watch the paragon of flying grace
Soaring through clouds to his aerie space.
King of the sky, his lordly mien
Is seldom matched on this earthly scene.
Far above turmoil, he glides content
While we, below, struggle in dissent.
We fight over jobs, debt and health;
Anxious and angry, obsessed with wealth.
We forget lessons from times gone by.
So, look once more to the king of the sky.
As his goal becomes set his keen eye sees
The perils and prizes that hide among trees.
Knowing the dangers he must reckon,
He also considers rewards that beckon.
When he plunges, it is never from greed.
He takes only what his growing brood needs.
He seeks no insurance against tomorrow;
Has not one hedge against pain and sorrow.
He lives each day as God has allowed
As happily as possible with head unbowed.
We call him king of all he surveys,
So, what might we learn from the regal ways
Of the eagle?

Ronald R. Hamilton
Sun City, AZ

[Hometown] Evansville, IN; [DOB] May 6, 1932; [Ed] BA, BD, MDiv, DPhil; [Occ] United Methodist minister; [Hobbies] reading, writing, traveling; [GA] my family

Birthday Blues

I woke up this morning facing the truth.
Okay lady—today is no spoof!
No use to think you can be defying,
Back off—hold tight—no use in crying.
Check your calendar, it's not lying,
Seen in black and white, no denying.

Wishing won't change anything,
The number "84" has a loud ring.
Get up out of bed old lady and sing,
You're still here, so ding-ding.
Laugh-love-hope-cheer
another year—sighing.

Nedra S. Moe
Winston, OR

[Hometown] Akron, OH; [DOB] February 10; [Ed] high school, two years college; [Occ] retired receptionist; [Hobbies] singing, dancing, reading, writing; [GA] traveling every U.S. state but one, many countries in Europe

I woke up at 6:00 a.m. on my birthday, by 7:00 a.m. I jumped out of bed with "Birthday Blues" ready to write down. It will always be a memorable birthday. Hopefully it won't be the last poem I write, though my creative juices are fading lately. I started writing in 1960s. I am the mother of four sons and one daughter, grandmother of six grandchildren, and great-grandmother of two. The other "grand" period of my life were the years I spent in "Sweet Adelines Chorus" stage shows—1950s and '60s—then traveling from 1970s to early 1990s in Europe, Hawaii, and the Caribbean. Many happy years!

Duck Disaster

Busy traffic snarled
Bumper to bumper
A tiny duck darted
Into traffic followed
By a swirl of fluffy yellow ducklings
Like yellow Easter candy
Blindly following mother
Into Capilano road congestion
Then toward the safety
Of the lush green forest
And back into traffic
Going this way and that
Mindlessly switching direction
On the narrow ledge of disaster.
Then I saw on the pavement
A crushed yellow pancake
As the duck and ducklings
Swirled and twirled
Around it until I rushed out
And herded them into the forest
To the applause and honks
And thumbs up of watching drivers
But there is no joy in my heart.
The mother duck is not the only one
Who knows how it feels
To lose a little duckling.

Gordon Roback
Vancouver, BC Canada

[Hometown] Montreal, BC; [DOB] February 26, 1952; [Ed] BA, MFA, MA, PhD, LLB; [Occ] starving writer; [Hobbies] building shacks in the woods; [GA] my three sons

Born in Montreal to a large, loud, loving family, I earned a BA with first class honours from McGill, an MA in English literature from the University of Toronto, and a law degree from UBC. I also earned an MFA and a PhD in film from the University of Southern California. I was recently awarded a first prize gold medal for the poem "All the Same" from the International Poetry Movement. My first book of poetry, When I think of You and Other Poems *can be found at Amazon.com.*

Make You Believe

I baited my hook and cast my line;
I fished in a sea, miles and miles wide.
So many took the bait, but still I had to decline.
For it just never felt right inside.

I was looking for someone to brighten my days
in their very own special ways.
At that time, little did I know
that it would start with your hello.

Our acquaintance has been brief,
but I hope to make you believe:
in yourself and happily-ever-after,
and hellos that don't end in disaster.

Amanda Pidlisny
Chateauguay, QC Canada

[Hometown] *Ste-Catherine, QC;* [DOB] *September 8, 1994;* [Ed] *modern language;* [Occ] *student;* [Hobbies] *poetry, photography, sports, scrapbooking*

I grew up in Ste-Catherine, Quebec. I am nineteen years old and recently graduated from the modern languages program at Dawson College. My hobbies include poetry, photography, scrapbooking and sports, such as horseback riding, volleyball, badminton and soccer. I also enjoy learning new languages. I speak English, French, Spanish, German and Italian, and I want to learn Greek and Portuguese. My greatest achievement has been overcoming anorexia nervosa. This poem was written for my boyfriend to let him know I want to be the one to make him believe in love again.

Misunderstood Feelings

She says she's fine, but she's going insane.
She says she feels good, but is in a lot of pain.
Says its nothing, when its really a lot.
Says she's okay, but she's not.

Shanissa Neufeldt
Edmonton, AB Canada

My name is Shanissa Neufeldt, and I live in Edmonton, AB. I am a people watcher and so most of my poems come from what I see on people's faces or what I notice from being so close to my friends. I haven't written many poems yet, but that is because I cannot just sit around and try and make one up, they just come to mind when I see something inspiring.

Hope

Airy white clusters in scattered disarray
loom from above
making food for a dove
or cardinal or jay
never knowing their worth,
donning hope for the day.

Helena M. Langley
Granite City, IL

Epic Mosquito Quatrain

Thy wicked ardor amazed thy Guy De Maupassant
Month of July, as thy hemophiliac
Mosquito illuminated scansion to thy big elephant
With amphibrach Ca-Cum-Ca nonchalant
Relevancy!

Bozana Belokosa
Pasadena, CA

The Storm

A ship being tossed about the sea
As water rages on both sides
I wanting to sound the alarm to flee
A ship, I just want to get to the other side
I want land before I capsize
I don't want to sink into the ocean below
Where nobody will find me floating
My engine has died and left me alone
The waves are battering me left and right
I can't hold on much longer, in this storm
Mayday! Mayday! a hole in my shell
Thunder and lightning, my radio just died
Not a soul to rescue me
Helpless am I all alone in this raging hell
I have come as far as I can
I am tired and lost in the storm of life
A brilliant light seeks me from the sky
I am tired and weak to journey no further
My nose looked up to land ahead
I think I can! I think I can!
And I did, thanks to the clearing storm
I will once again find my way to the sea
As for my captain, he was washed away
He as my captain, and I as his ship

Donna McDiarmid
Welland, ON Canada

[Hometown] Welland, ON; [DOB] June 1, 1960; [Ed] ninth grade; [Occ] homemaker; [Hobbies] puzzles, poetry; [GA] motherhood

I am a mother of two daughters and have been married to my husband for thirty years. I was fourteen when I began writing. Writing is a place of fairy tales where you can exist without someone trying to find you—lost in time, giving life to a talking ship, where I become one with it. I have full control of its destiny. Poetry is one thing in my life that showed me my purpose. Believe me, we all need a place to hide: Poetry is mine.

So It Is

S shaped grooves
created by my mower yesterday.
It's overcast.
Maybe rain, maybe not.
Sprinkler twirls and swirls.
My thoughts prance.
Three children I had,
They have all gone bad.
Haven't received a call
nor a card for five years now.
Sprinkler twirls and swirls.
My children attempted
a destructive calamity.
They were met with
confounded resiliency.
Storm is in the past
and reposes to the last.
Done my war with fire ants.
Done my war with kids.
Fly is in my wine.
It's all benign.
Sprinkler twirls and swirls.

Bonnie Culver
Fritch, TX

Born January 12, 1943 in Cleveland, OH. I am a post-graduate educated in life science and currently retired in the Texas Panhandle. I'm well traveled and lived in several states due to job transfer. My favorite poet is Robert Frost. I love the rhythm of the rhyme and have trouble getting away from it, so I combined it with prose. I have no knowledge of poetry writing but have been published off and on since high school.

A Mom to Many

In childhood,
We did not have much;
You see, we were quite poor.
But my mother,
She gave us her love—
and we could never require more.

She kept us warm,
And fed,
and dry;
She did the best that she could do.
She never worried about herself,
Though now,
She knows she should.

She still gives us all her love,
Her heart is so big
And warm.
Now she had made our house a home,
For those who require more.

Kayla Tellier
Surrey, BC Canada

[Hometown] Surrey, BC; [DOB] December 24, 1994; [Ed] high school; [Occ] movie/TV extra; [Hobbies] *writing, reading, acting, dancing, sports; [GA] the first poem I got published*

Growing up, my sister and I always seemed to attract the type of kid who needed help—whether it was a roof to go over his or her head where he or she wouldn't be abused, or just being someone who could offer support. My mom was always the one who took them under her wings; there has always been room in her heart and our home for children in trouble, and that's why my mom is my role model: the one I want to be like when I grow up. She truly is the best mom in the world—not just to us, but to others too.

Tomorrow?

I'm eighty-four, old enough to look back
Are there things I need to do
Address my wrongs and try to atone
And looking forward to plan my way
Are finances in order and bills to be paid
Doing things tomorrow should not be my game
If it's bright and sunny why not play
And put work off for another day
A message to all regardless of age
After the important things are done
Many tomorrows are most welcome

John Atz
Jacksonville, FL

[Hometown] Jacksonville, FL; [DOB] April 17, 1929; [Ed] BSBA University of Florida; [Occ] Insurance underwriter; [Hobbies] greyhound racing; [GA] passed both seventh and eighth grades in the same year

Life has been a challenge. Wins and losses are part of the game. I could have done better but I'm pleased with the results. Give me a C+.

The Miserable Blizzard

An unforgettable day in time,
one call at six-thirty on a cold winter's morn
that changed the lives of so many.
As the snow began to fall,
we drove to you faster and faster.
The harder we drove, the more snowflakes that fell.
Why this day?
I believe that the angels' feathers
were falling from the heavens above.
Are they making a bed
for you, on this day in time?
As minutes turned into hours,
inches turned into a foot of snow
surrounding the ground we stood on.
I watched my world turn
upside down, as day went to night.
Your breath is slowing down now,
slower and slower.
As I hold your hands
tight and wait
(take your time).
For you may go now, it's okay.
The angel's are here, they're
among us, Nanny!
Make your journey home, now!
Remember our love for you
will always remain.
For today and tomorrow
it just stopped snowing!

Michelle L. Hamlett
Hopewell, VA

[Hometown] Hopewell, VA; [DOB] October 29, 1968; [Ed] high school; [Occ] housewife; [Hobbies] writing, fishing, camping, reading; [GA] my three children

I live in Hopewell, VA. I am a mother of three children, a wife of twenty-seven years, and a grandmother of six. I was inspired to write this poem for my mother-in-law. She was my best friend, my mother when I needed her to be, and a loving person, mother, and wife herself. She became very ill all of the sudden in February of 2010. She passed away on February 10, 2010. I know in my heart she is with God and all of His angels. She was everyone's nanny!

The Painted Smile

Shades of pink and orange and red
So many ways to hide the dread

So begins the painted smile

Complaining about your frizzy hair
When in reality, the cupboard is bare

Flash that pretty, painted smile

It's only dust gone in your eye
When deep inside, you just want to die

Keep up your painted, little smile

Hide the tears, night after night
The punishment's only worse if you fight

Keep it up, bear it proud, wear it like a holy shroud

That pretty, little painted smile

Rachelle Fried
King of Prussia, PA

[Hometown] King of Prussia, PA; [Occ] stylist; [GA] sharing my poetry with the world

It's Better Late Than Never

Adopting the old adage, "It's better late than never"
Is especially true in certain situations
Just how many times have you said
I'll call my old childhood friend Molly today, if I get the chance
But you often shrug your weary shoulders
And become a classic couch potato
Too often, your innermost desires are put on the back shelf
Then one day, a loud knock comes on the door
It's a telegram from Christina, Molly's daughter—your goddaughter
Molly has suddenly and peacefully passed away
Your tender heart becomes ever so heavy with deep, sincere grief
Tears just seem to flow incessantly; you say to yourself
O God, why did I put off calling Molly, time after time?
We were friends in our youth and through the Great Depression
If I had a crust of bread, so did she...especially when
Every man and woman were for themselves and God was for us all
Hoover's economic collapse caused both of us to humbly scrub floors
for fifty cents, a banana, and a can of mustard sardines
I have faith in the Holy Spirit's promise that I will see Molly
Once again, Jehovah continues to assure me—His loyal one—
That Molly and I will experience a brand new spiritual resurrection
A real-life rendezvous on judgment day...for now, I will keep hope alive
It's better late than never

Naomi Abdulrahman
Joppa, MD

I was inspired to write "It's Better Late Than Never" as a reflection of a true-life, inspirational story about two women of color during the Great Depression in the 1930s and '40s. One of these courageous women was my maternal grandmother, Margaret, and the other stout-hearted lady was her friend Molly. They learned how to use two very important tools in order to survive: sharing and bonding. If my grandmother had a slice of bread and Molly didn't, she would break the bread and share it unconditionally. No reunion between the two ever took place, and Molly has passed away.

God's Peace

Ethnic background or color
of skin has nothing to do with the soul within.
We all want war and conflict to cease.
We all desire world peace
God's peace is there for one and all
When we follow the Master's call
Christ laid down his life for one and all
He never said our road would be smooth or easy
He promised I will never leave thee
God's eternal love is sweet and sure
In God's hands we are secure
When we cross the great divide
Loving arms open wide
no pain or sorrow can enter there
God's peace and love we all will share

John Brannick
Colby, KS

Long Road to Success

My long road to success made me think about childhood, when I said I was going to be successful. My long road to success made me shed tears and made me emotional, because I thought about all the rough moments of my life. My long road to success made me brave and confident. My long road to success was overwhelming and painful. It wasn't easy but I didn't want to give up. I was unsure and hopeless. I also had mixed feelings. I felt like crying. I felt like crying away my pain. But I said I won't stop. Now I'm successful to have accomplished my goals. Now I can be an inspiration for people who experienced what I have been through. Just know there is hope and dreams do come true. Just think positive.

Malik Gayden
Rochester, NY

[Hometown] Rochester, NY; [DOB] February 28, 1991; [Ed] graduated; [Hobbies] poetry, dancing, making my short films; [GA] graduating from high school in 2012

My name is Malik. I've been writing poetry for exactly seven years now. It really keeps me motivated and helps me express my feelings. I really enjoy writing poetry. I'm very passionate about it. I also like inspiring others with my poetry and talent because it puts a big smile on my face. That's the most beautiful highlight of poetry. My goal is to start my own homeless charity if I win this contest. I love and admire helping others. I am so grateful and blessed to share my new poem with you guys. Thank you for this amazing opportunity.

Eber & Wein Publishing

My Friends

Many years ago
You came into my life;
Little did we know
You'd bring me such delight.

As each day goes by
With all we have to do,
I wonder with a sigh
What would I do without you!

The time so swiftly passes
Never knowing what each day will bring;
You always keep me laughing,
Leaving thoughts that make me sing.

It always makes life bright
I know without a doubt,
Having good friends in sight
Is what life is all about!

I thank the Lord each minute
Of every passing day;
For having you in it
Means more than I can say!

Daisyann Fredericks
Canajoharie, NY

[Hometown] Canajoharie, NY; [DOB] January 27, 1935; [Ed] twelfth grade, clerical work; [Occ] PT clerical bank, sewing; [Hobbies] make two hundred of my own Christmas cards; [GA] quilt making

I'm a widowed mom of four children: three girls and one boy! I still work part time at a local bank operations center, and I also make quilts along with pillows, pot holders, etc. I also do dressmaking and alterations of all sorts. I was fortunate to have taken a hot air balloon ride with my youngest daughter and youngest grandson. I was surprised to join my daughter on a cruise from New York City to Bermuda this year for seven days. I have a lot of wonderful friends—they inspire some of my poems. I also have two great-grandsons!

Love Once Again

I was asked: If I could do "anything"
What would I do?
I would go back in time
Just so I could be with you

To hold you, to love you
To have you hold me
To love once again
To set my heart free

I walk around each day
Hurt and so confused
Wondering why this had to happen
Now not knowing what to do

But I hope in time
When I walk through Heaven's Gate
We both can love once again
Together in this godly place

Kenneth L. Combs
Pahrump, NV

[Hometown] Pahrump, NV; [DOB] October 5, 1962; [Ed] high school graduate, degree in business law; [Occ] retired from the army

I started writing in 2005. I was at work, thumbing through a magazine, when I saw a contest for poetry, so I entered it. Since then, I have been published in four different books; I have also published my own book called Writings of Life and Heartfelt Memories. *The good Lord has given me this gift, and I am very thankful. I feel blessed every day to be able to share my work with the world.*

I'm Going Home

I'm going home finally.
July ninth they told me
I had the Big C ...
Now I'm going to be
with the only man
who truly loved and
believed in me ...
For he's in Heaven waiting
and will now be coming down
sending for me.
I'm leaving Hell
and going to the Kingdom
of love, peace, and happiness,
where that fits my personality.
No more pain or tears or hurt
that I bear,
I will finally be flying high with the angels
in the celestial lights in God's Kingdom,
and once again I will be free!

Dianna L. Bulisky
East Lansdowne, PA

I lost my fiance eleven years ago and this poem is based on him being my guardian angel and coming for me when it's my time! For he is the only man who believed in everything I did in life and saw it through before his life was taken against his will. And I do believe he's always with me and I pray he'll see me through this horrible turmoil I'm going through!

Mother Did You Ever Take the Time to Realize

Mother did you ever take the time to realize
How much pain that I was already in

Mother did you ever take the time to realize
How much I already had on me

Mother did you ever take the time to realize
How selfish and inconsiderate you are to me

Mother did you ever take the time to realize
How much emotional distress you have
Subjected me to most of my life

Mother did you ever take the time to realize
That you don't really care about how bad you treat me
When I'm down or how it makes me feel

Mother did you ever take the time to realize
That you never ask me how I feel instead
You just project your feelings onto me.

Well I have and I've been praying for you
Mother that the Lord Jesus will enlighten your conscience
So that you can *realize* one day in your life
And you will take the time to care because I've
Already forgiven you for everything that you've done to me
In my life.

LaTonya A. Seabrooks
Sacramento, CA

[Hometown] Sacramento, CA; [DOB] May 19, 1967; [Ed] Culinary Arts; [Occ] Caregiver; [Hobbies] Watching sports and listening to music; [GA] being published

I was inspired to write this poem because I wanted to use it to encourage anyone who has been mistreated by someone to show them mercy by being kind in spite of the way they have been treated by that person. We all make mistakes and errors in our way of thinking. Even though I've grown and progressed in my spirituality, my mother hasn't and I'm hoping and praying that she will see the pain that she has brought on me and treat me right before she or I leave this earthly journey. Forgiveness is powerful.

The God Particle

"A thousand years is but a day."
Time is the truest cornerstone of reality.
An enigma that hides the secret of "always was and always will be."
A peculiar twist of its nature seemingly brings forth creation from nothingness, yet it was always
    there.
In truth, there was never nothingness.
A circle of causality we can scarcely fathom—a paradoxical genesis that reflects the divine nature
    seen in prophesy throughout the Bible.
You can look for a particle all you like. The truly wise know that in this mortal realm, "Light" behaves differently when it is observed.
Everything we see and think we measure is but a shadow without substance.
There is a truth and a reality that goes beyond what is seen through the eyes of science.
It lies with God and His word which speaks through the ages of what will be… as if it were
    yesterday.
All things can be made new. From never ending to never ending, love and peace can reign forever.
Two ways have been placed before us.
You are free to choose what you will allow your heart to embrace.
I can only remind you, "Before the foundation of world, Jesus Christ knew you."
There is still time for you to finally know Him… and the love that makes eternity worth living!

John Zarbo
Painesville, OH

Longing for Home

My heart knows an emptiness—

A hunger for what used to be:
    Familiar streets and favorite parks,
    Places laden with memories,
    Even routine tasks, such as
        mowing the grass,
        shoveling the walks,
        dealing with garbage,
    Speak of home, and add to the "never again" ache.

The loss of special moments…
    with the kids,
    with friends,
    with co-workers,
Creates a vacuum and a hunger for what once was and is no more.

I know that all things change, cannot be duplicated or retrieved,
    Yet I thirst for what once was,
        is no more,
            and never will be again—

Yes, I am longing for *home*!

Mary K. Himens
Champaign, IL

[Hometown] Antioch, IL; [DOB] September 24, 1929; [Ed] PhD in pastoral counseling; [Occ] psychotherapist; [Hobbies] reading, writing prose and poetry, sewing, ; [GA] alumni of the two Universities where I was employed, have a named scholarship, and the wing of a building in my name

As a professed religious woman, I have experienced a very rich and rewarding life of service—as a teacher, principal, parish worker, campus minister, and college professor. This listing does not include my many years as a psychotherapist in private practice. My poetry and other writings have been published in various journals, as well as my own volume of poetry, Images: Sights and Insights. The poem above was written at the request of a recently divorced gentlemen who had been a client for a number of years. He said it confirmed the aches in his heart for all that had been "his home," and soothed that heart by naming them.

Maybe

I'm scared for my life!
My mind is racing and not only am I thinking once but twice

My heart is pumping! Pumping very fast the fluid
Life has made me do things, that I never thought I'd be doing

So they say I need some help but no one wants to do it
Rotting in jail is where they want me, instead of in a institution

Careful is how I live or you can call it paranoia
I'm telling you this information right now so you don't say I never told ya

Be busy looking over my shoulders, thinking way too many thoughts
My fingers are closed very tightly (into knuckles), in case I might get caught

With a sneak peek or a low blow
Too many decisions to make nowadays and I don't know which way to go

I betcha danger will be there, seems it loves me more than me
Running out of options right now and every single chance that I receive

So what is it that I am saying? That I think I might be crazy
Or maybe there's something missing in my life and that's what really seems to phase me

Or maybe something needs to happen that will sneakily just amaze me
Or maybe losing my destroyed life is what I am - secretly - quietly - craving

Jonathan Rodriguez
Union City, NJ

Problems Today

Where did our freedom go, right before our eyes?
Our government keeps finding ways,
All we hear from them are lots of lies.
So much fighting in our government, it's so sad—
This force takes from the people and never gives back.
Just so much wrong that is going on and so much bad,
So much devastation in the world today.
Our government helps every country but our own—
So many jobless, homeless and starving right here at home.
A government that just keeps shutting programs down,
And those people in government just think it's okay
To just throw this country away.
A government that won't work together to get along…
So many people out of work for ever so long.
They gave tax breaks to companies to move to other countries.
Most people are living paycheck to paycheck;
I sure blame our government, by heck.
A real need to eliminate the career politician, for sure:
Eliminate the IRS, with a flat tax for part of a cure.
Start taking care of the people who pay their bills,
'Cause we sure need to cure this country's ills.
The way God wanted the world to be…
God intended everything for you and me.
God bless America!

Deanna Maria Bacon
Colona, IL

[Hometown] Davenport, IA; [DOB] March 21, 1943; [Ed] collegiate courses; [Occ] retired from position as unit supervisor, ACA; [Hobbies] sewing, crafts, poetry, gardening, reading; [GA] Who's Who Midwest and Who's Who American Women

I was born in Davenport, IA in 1943 and won the title of Miss Davenport at the age of four. I learned a lot growing up and became the first female production unit supervisor with Aluminum Company of America in 1977. I made it into Who's Who in America in the Midwest in 1992 and Who's Who in American Women in 1993. I am now retired and free to write poetry. I wrote this poem because I feel our government is taking this country's people for a bad ride to nowhere. I worked hard for everything I have and am not willing to give it to politicians.

Dedications

Dressing environments prettily,
Smiling to folk sweetly,
Ignoring envious storm's hate,
America roses rely on energetic sunlight.

Building colorful worlds,
Presenting milky syrup to residents,
Resisting diseases and bitter winters,
Canadian maple trees possess vigorous trucks.

Curing of illness of monarchs,
Tolerating woman discrimination pains,
Struggling against corrupt officials,
Great Jang Geum was founding her immovable ambitions.

Carrying back Sanskrit sutra refinement,
Dealing with evil beauties' harassment,
Fighting monsters of pilgrimage expedition,
Tang Sanzang was burying himself in the pious persuasion

Xubao Zhang
Kitchener, ON Canada

[Hometown] Chengdu in China; [Ed] PhD; [Occ] engineer; [Hobbies] writing poems, gardening; [GA] national science and technology progress prize

I wrote this poem to admire some of the beauties of nature, which change our world image, such as Americas roses making the environment more beautiful and Canadian maple trees producing syrup to benefit people. I also admire a few ancient persons who brought huge benefits to societies. Jang Geum was a top Korean medical lady in the Joseon dynasty, and emperor Jungjong granted her title Great. Xuanzang (title Sanzang) was the most famous Chinese monk in the Tang dynasty, adopted brother of the emperor Taizong because he took back Hinduism scripture to China.

Wrong Way

The world is full of hate and war
With crowds of people near and far
All shouting threats of violence.

We long for peace and happiness
But here at home we're on our knees
Praying for the wars to cease.

We're helpless as we long for peace
While sending youngsters out of reach
To distant shores of mixed-up strangers.

The world's not caring anymore
Where is the love religions teach?
Complete destructions' within reach!
I fear!

Juanita Weber
Florissant, MO

[Hometown] Florissant, MO; [DOB] August 28, 1930; [Ed] public schools, some college; [Occ] being a mother, hardest job; [Hobbies] reading, bowling; [GA] traveling world and US

I read the newspaper every day, and most news upsets me. These words in my verse woke me up at four in the morning.

Tracks You Leave

Walk softly, my brothers all,
Feel Mother Earth's soil
beneath your feet.
Listen to the wind,
Study the stars at night,
Watch brother crow fly above.
Remember we all have one creator.
Be generous to those in need,
Have a kind word to speak,
May the path of peace
be your guide.

Compose a happy song,
Pen a verse of praise, gratitude,
Help a friend far away.
The journey you take today
Leaves tracks for tomorrow's
children to follow.
Keep peace and love in your heart,
You shall be remembered
by the tracks you leave.

Andrew Batcho
McAdoo, PA

[Hometown] McAdoo, PA; [DOB] November 13, 1945; [Ed] college graduate; [Occ] wide variety; [Hobbies] writing and scrapbooking; [GA] U.S. Navy four years

I was born and raised in McAdoo, PA and retired in 2007. My spare time is spent writing, following Native American Indian interests and caring for my Shih Tzu.

Lillian

Lillian laid there stiffly in bed
As I listened attentively to every
Word she said.

The awful disease of arthritis had
Invaded her body at an early age
And now in her forties she was
In such a crippling stage.

She endured much pain and suffering
Without a frown on her face
'Cause she believed strongly
In God's ever-loving grace.

There was never any sign of
Bitterness in her heart
And with praise and Thanksgiving
Her day would start.

She may not have been able with
Me to walk, run, or play
But she taught me many skills and valuable
Lessons that have greatly helped me
Along life's way.

Carolyn Councilman
Graham, NC

[Hometown] Roxboro, NC; [DOB] October 7, 1947; [Ed] community college graduate; [Occ] nurse (retired after forty years); [Hobbies] crafts, writing, and leadership roles; [GA] lifetime of service to others

At a very early age, I was given the opportunity to work with a lady who was crippled with arthritis. Lillian taught me how to soak her hands in paraffin, administer meds, assist with physical therapy, and how to transfer her from bed to chair with the use of a hydraulic lift. Together we also wrote the neighborhood news for our local newspaper. Most importantly, she taught me about Jesus and encouraged me to attend church. Other than my parents, she had the greatest influence on my life and so my poem entitled "Lillian" is written in her memory.

Life

The sky opens to blue
It's the beginning of the show
My eyes adjust to dawn's new light
The first act begins, I know
Every person, plant and creature
Awaken to their part
The sounds of day are music
The surroundings supply the art
My body moves, the sun appears as
Gentle breezes blow
The second act continues, and
Life's expressions flow
Ever changing seasons provide
Summer's heat to winter's snow.

Linda M. Coppola
Seminole, FL

It is such a pleasure to have my poetry read and considered for publication. I am somewhat retired, living in Florida with my husband and yellow lab Sunshine. Thank you for this opportunity.

Mother

Life has ended

and still I know the
sun will shine tomorrow

come the night the moon
will glow bright and
the stars still twinkle

and in my grief, I will
learn to live without you.

Julie A. Gravel
San Diego, CA

I am a middle-aged female, I have a husband, a dog, and five cats. Although I am a very private person I do like to write. The only work I ever had shared was in a school newspaper, it was short-lived fame but it was fun. My mother's passing inspired this poem.

Oblivion: The Big Sleep

Absence of life, love, and sorrow, can't make me sad.
Things will disappear, I won't remember what I had.
Now, too much silence walls closing in.
I won't miss places I've been.
Each day as the one before, I welcome sounds of rain.
Silent snow continuous white. No birds call I welcome night.
No dreams just sweet sleep, no pain to waken me.
No longing for what I missed in life, my soul free.
After I'm gone if loved ones suffer I won't know,
for oblivion will spare me this very final blow.
I've had a long run long enough I say,
It's getting harder to remember my last good day.
I've reached a place where words I know fail
to stay in my brain long enough to prevail.
This burdens me. I long in the night to write thoughts
down before they disappear with morning light.
Reading passed the hours of solitude for me,
transferring me to places where I couldn't be.
I won't be able to miss voices heard laughter from the past,
Joy and pleasures I knew couldn't last.
I can't miss a furry friend now following me around,
from chair to bed soft paws making no sound.
I still count blessings especially three.
What I've given children they return to me.
Yes Oblivion the big sleep will be fine.
I stumbled often but got up, a few rewards were mine.

Betty Tenney
Sterling Heights, MI

I'm a senior, not over the hill but getting very close to the top at eighty-five. Since I still have poetry, stories, and songs scrambling around in my head faster than I get them on paper, I can't sit in a rocking chair yet. I've had a career in painting and teaching art for fifty years. In between this and raising three children, I wrote novels, kids' stories, poetry, and songs. Getting published is a tough nut to crack and more than a full-time endeavor, which I started too late in life. I must say it still gives me much pleasure in my old age.

Reverse Skydiving

It sounds quite insane
I start from the ground and land in the plane
It's a new sport that's going around
The shoot opens and whoosh— off the ground!
A few seconds of gravity-free air
I enter the plane with hardly a care
If you don't believe me
You will see
I need a great check on reality!

Marvin D. Goldfarb
Sunnyside, NY

[Hometown] Sunnyside, NY; [DOB] January 20, 1939; [Ed] two years college; [Occ] retired; [Hobbies] poetry and photography; [GA] emcee and host Kew Garden's Community Center

Marvin Goldfarb has been writing since the age of twelve and has written over 4,000 poems. He has performed all over NYC and has established his reputation at such venues as the NY Poetry Forum Airman Club, Cadman Park Plaza Restaurant (The Poets of the Round Table), YW/MHA of Forest Hills and the Kew Gardens Community Center (KGCC). He hosts "Show Us Your Talent" at the KGCC monthly show. Mr. Goldfarb has had three poems published by Eber & Wein Publishing, which included "Who Is This Admirer?," "My Cat Says," and "Marvin the Millionaire." A fourth poem published by Great Poets Across America, which is called "Moses Gets the Ten Commandments," won an award. Also, on Create Space he published the poem "My Who Family."

Seaside Splendor

In the erupting fullness of each mesmerizing cloud
It seems the patterns that form are screaming to be found
Nothing below apart from emerald's ocean glow
Vast magic spreads with every wave that grows
Imagination is a glorious pool
But this wide open space is nobody's fool
Show her respect with every glance
Never taking for granted her massive stance
Many have lingered in her loving arms
Forever changed by such elegance and charm
Words are left unspoken, for none can truly express
These feelings she evokes of unsurpassed blissfulness

Sami Korientz
Santa Maria, CA

[Hometown] Santa Maria, CA; [DOB] April 12, 1959; [Ed] high school, three years college; [Occ] poet, artist; [Hobbies] writing, reading, laughing; [GA] mother, wife, grandnana

Since a very young age, I have written poetry and short stories. Refusing to let disabilities define me, I have worked hard to hone in on the things that make me feel fulfilled. Expressing myself through my poetry is one of the most exhilarating feelings I have ever experienced. I am a newlywed, at age fifty-four. My wonderful husband, CK, is the guiding force behind me. His love and encouragement continuously spur me on to pursue my passion for writing poetry. We live an enriching life on the central coast of California.

Caring Hands

The vocation you have chosen
To serve others with caring,
To give of yourself completely
And to warm hearts by sharing.

You are not always appreciated
Takin' advantage of, so often,
While working long, hard continuous hours
With most of your patients, spoiled rotten.

Some of you have husbands and children
And must keep up with work and home,
Many are working just to keep up
And exhausted, go home to be alone.

It takes a special person
To hold someone's hand while dying,
To tell a child, I know you can, and smile
When deep in your heart, you're crying.

Take pride in all that you do
God has blessed you with those hands,
He will hold you close to his heart
But your patients are your biggest fans.

Shirley Cole
Dickinson, TX

The Shining Light

I look up to the sky
And see the sun
Glowing like a bright streak
And I wonder why
It seems so bright
Like a "shining light."
I feel it beckoning to me
To let me know if I can see
What brightens up the world
The light! Billowing like a swirl
Of golden streaks
Heaped up in yellow peaks.
I want to know it all
So I can understand the wall
Of light that falls from Heaven above
Shimmering, swirling, flying
And soft like a beautiful dove.
I feel so fine
It's like I had a design
To make the world a better place
For everyone and every race
I ask you all
To look up at the sun
And you will see
A wonderful world in which to be.

Harriet David
Richmond, VA

[Hometown] Richmond, VA; [DOB] January 14, 1937; [Ed] associate's degree—Human SVS, one and a half years toward bachelor's degree; [Occ] retired human rights advocate for juvenile delinquents; [Hobbies] writing poems; [GA] raising three great kids

Survivor Tree

A cloud of black covers the sky
The Twin Towers give way
The world is stunned, wondering why
On this most fateful day

Almost three thousand lives taken
From such a hateful crime
Our sense of security is shaken
Healing will take some time

Beneath the wreckage and rubble
A damaged Pear was found
A tree in serious trouble
Would turn it all around

With blackened trunk and branches burned
The tree had almost died
Trapped below heavy steel, interned
A wonder it survived

Later planted at Ground Zero
With love and tender care
Honoring each fallen hero
So many come to stare

A lone Pear among Swamp White Oaks
Standing thirty feet tall
Many emotions it evokes
A sign of hope for all

Emily Krusos
Huntington, NY

[Hometown] Huntington, NY; [DOB] November 4, 1998; [Ed] Cold Spring Harbor High School; [Occ] student; [Hobbies] swimming; [GA] competing in the NY State Swimming Championships

Being from New York, the terrorist attack on 9/11 was especially devastating. Since family friends lost a loved one in the devastation, we visited the memorial at Ground Zero to honor his memory. Along the edge of the waterfalls stands a lone Callery Pear tree among a host of Swamp White Oaks. When I learned about its moving story, I was inspired to write "Survivor Tree," a poem of hope in the face of tragedy.

Explain

Where do eagles build their nests?
What do we use to stand time's tests?
One who died saved us all
Upon His name we often call

One who did only good
Died upon a piece of wood
With Him a thief stole paradise
A penitent heart his merchandise

Was this world made all by chance?
Better take another glance
Miracles on Earth abound
Witnessed here by sight or sound

Scientific age of heros
Covering the Earth with zeros
We are given our own choice
Do we listen to His voice?

Do you believe this is a place
That floats forever through the space?
By accidental chance was wrought?
Falsely proven by your thought!

Kenneth Hinkle
Winchester, VA

Choices

We all make choices...some good, some bad
Some choices are made on information we've had
Some choices are made on what we desire
We've heard lectures that tend to inspire
"Follow your dreams," no matter what!
"If I can do it, you can do it"...we've heard that a lot!
Talents and abilities are different, it's true
What's right for me may not be right for you
With a physical disability, use what you need
To help you perform and help you succeed
If you cannot compete, or don't want to, be true
Let others know what you can and can't do
I cannot compete in a race that is run
Others try to convince me to race 'cause it's fun
But because of my lungs, I can't do it
So, let me be truthful: Stop putting me through it!
Be respectful of others, and don't lie to yourself
Make choices that help assist you and your health

Carol Kaufman
Portland, OR

Mid Winter in Michigan

Here it is, late January again
We've had our mid-winter thaw
Hardly any snow so far, we're really due
For a big sock in the jaw

Today we're getting lake effect
Tomorrow a clipper's blowin' through
That'll pile the white stuff up
And make things hard to do

The drifts are now apiling up
The plow man filled my drive
I had just finished clearing it out
If I could catch him, he'd get skinned alive!

The icicles are a-forming
The cold nips at our toes
All I want is a blazing fire
And some bobbing marshmallows

The wife is on the sofa, curled in a blanket, cozy warm
The cat's asleep in the corner, waiting out the storm
Me, I'm finally in my lazy boy, a hot toddy next to me
Soft music on the stereo, very soon, asleep I'll be.

Charles P. Foley Sr.
Rockford, MI

[Hometown] Rockford, MI; [DOB] December 23, 1950; [Ed] Journey Millwright—J. electrician; [Occ] maintenance and part-time cook; [Hobbies] cooking and wood working; [GA] becoming a master mason

I'm usually moved to write by what goes on around me. As I've gotten older, I'm not outside like I used to be. Weather and the people I'm with seem to be the trigger. I like to write about happy things. Doom and gloom is just not my style.

The Pain of Rain

Some may say the rain comes from pain,
that the rain may be the cause of your pain;
but whatever you may go through,
just remember that after the rain
there is something more to gain.

The rain that comes from all of one's pain
comes to bring you peace, but realize:
what you know as to where the fault lies
is where the pain of rain can wash away all of one's blame.

God gives us rain because of the pain one has,
and He also gives us sunshine to let us know that He's still alive.

So knowing that the rain comes from something which is uncontrollable,
one should blame the real reason for one's shame;
and remember that God has all power to control one's gain.

Latisa D. Hubbard
Lynchburg, VA

[Hometown] Brookneal, VA; [DOB] December 3, 1980; [Ed] certified legal administrator; [Occ] homemaker; [Hobbies] singing and writing; [GA] reaching goal after goal

Nature's Music

Fleetingly subtle the world whispers its song—
Shh, don't you hear it? It's there all day long.
Sometimes you can sense it, as life chimes along—
sighing willowy winds in lullaby song—
sometimes a faint moan as trees bend in dance
or subtle groan of Earth's ground, giving roots a fair chance.
The smooth baritone of a river, in its swift flowing flight,
singing praise to the sun for its glistening light.
Then comes crystal clear diamond sounds of shining stars out at night, chanting down an array
of
   twinkling delight.
The murmuring dark, quiet skies—before the yawn of daybreak—followed by a spectrum of
   color, in pastels galore—
as if casted by cymbals bursting forth evermore,
and our sunrise opens up to a sky we adore.
Then the sun soars in solo, with screaming bright light—
prelude to blue sky that hums in tune, with these sights.
You must sit back, look and listen—there's more to this song.
Nature's musical magic can go on and on.
Just listen and see an array of nature's sweet sounds—
a symphony of our existence—to be enjoyed all around.

Carol E. Gange
Baltimore, MD

[Hometown] Baltimore, MD; [DOB] July 17, 1945; [Ed] high school/business trade courses; [Occ] office manager/business accounting; [Hobbies] poetry, water color and ink art, and crafts; [GA] surviving stage four cancer

Trying to create elusive or subtle sounds to nature's natural things is challenging and desirably interesting. When the two flow easily together, some natural things do make sounds; others have to be left to the imagination that can only be seen by your mind's eye. It can be a very interesting game or hobby, and it creates a beautiful instinct of knowledge. This poem is dedicated to my children, David Russell and Carol Suz'an, who have always been God's gift of nature's music to me. I hope my poem is enjoyed by all

Gun Control Is People Control

The second amendment, the rights of Americans.
The common people's rights to keep and bear arms.
If you want to own firearms then own one.
If you don't want to own firearms then don't.
Our government gave all American's rights.
The F.B.I. says more people are killed or injured
by criminals using baseball bats than firearms.
The gun laws we have didn't stop
the Sandy Hook killings.
The gun laws we have are not obeyed,
not obeyed by the crazies or criminals or gang bangers.
The tax paying citizens and the NRA want people's rights.
Remember all criminals, militia, and crazies
choose to lose their legal rights,
to own or use firearms.
All the common man asks is to be treated fairly
All the legal hunter asks is to be allowed to hunt wildgame.
All the farmer asks is to be able to protect his family and farm.
All the police wish to do is protect all America's people.

Betty Ruth Tollefson
Bagley, MN

I'm a retired sixty-five-year-old woman. I enjoy writing poetry. I graduated in 1966 from Fillmore C-1 High School, Fillmore, MO. I trained and worked in the nursing field where I helped bring in life and helped as the battle of life ended. I've volunteered in different areas. My husband Jim and I enjoy fishing and collecting John Deere items. We believe there should be some gun control. I am a wife, and mother of hunters, veterans, farmers, police officers, and maintenance managers. They are all licensed gun carriers, to help protect themselves and others, or enjoy their hobbies.

Penny

Come little penny, please bring me some luck!
Admit it, I saved you, from out of the muck!
Your copper face shining, so new and so bright;
I couldn't ignore you—it just wasn't right!

From some careless wallet you fell, or were tossed.
Too lowly to bend for, you weren't worth the cost.
In grime and cold snow you were destined to lie,
Sorely kicked and down-trodden, by each passer-by.

Most people think you don't add up to much,
But here, in my pocket, you're warm to the touch.
For you, humble penny, were made to be spent,
Whether hoarded, or wasted, or borrowed, or lent.

It's the small things in life that count most in the end;
A birdsong, a snowflake, a penny, a friend.
Some human hand made you, and you have your place.
I could swear there's a smile now, each side of your face!

Valerie J. Palmer
Peace River, AB Canada

"Penny" was first written to honour the penny (originally made of copper, and called a "copper" in England!). Sadly, it has recently been banished from circulation, both in England, and here in Canada. Everyone now has jars of them sitting on a shelf somewhere! Since I grew up in the World War II era, in Britain, my father taught me to be thrifty, and to save every penny I found. (I did, and I still do!) This habit has extended into many other areas of my life, for which I thank my Dad.

I Am Me

I am me to control life
I am me to control my dreams
I am me that has a heart
I am me who cares
I am me that loves my two little brothers forever
I am me who is their big sissy
I have hope
I pray for everyone every day
My life is true
Some stuff is stuck to me like glue
I need to move on and bond with the true ones in the heart
I will change the ugly in me to beautiful as can be
Accept the awesome you that will grow through time
Wait and see
You are life I say thee
Amen

Jordan Elizabeth Bassett
Wasilla, AK

I am eighteen years old and am a fourth generation Alaskan. I love writing poetry, short stories, and songs. I also love music, singing, and sports, and have a good sense of humor.

Whitney

You are my sunshine
Granddaughter of mine.
You light up my days, you are special in so many ways.
You are nice, you are kind,
In children, nowadays that's hard to find,
Granddaughter of mine.
When it's raining I think of you.
Then the sun comes shining through, how I enjoy our
Whitney days.
I sit and count the ways; we shop till we drop,
Then we drink cold soda pop, we eat snacks and watch a movie.
It's really groovy.
You're ten and getting older, but still young enough to sit on my lap,
Your head on my shoulder.
We make cookies, we bake cakes
When we get tired we take breaks
Hurrah for Whitney days.
That's the way it should be just you and me,
Having all kinds of fun one on one.
You and Grandma on Whitney days.
You don't visit that often but when you do,
Grandma can't stop thinking of you.

Mary Rombout Andrus
Modesto, CA

[Hometown] Salida, CA; [DOB] August 18, 1939; [Ed] eighth grade; [Occ] laborer, cannery worker; [Hobbies] reading; [GA] being self-efficient

I started working at five years of age for a German family cutting fruit. Dad would drop me off at five in the morning and pick me up at five at night. When I was seven, my checks bought all the school clothes for me and my siblings, three younger and three older. I went to work when I was twelve at a cannery and also attended school from nine in the morning to three in the afternoon. Mother picked me up after school, and I would work at the cannery from four until after midnight. I got home and went to sleep, so I could go to school the next day. I worked in the cannery and with frozen foods for forty-six years, full time for the last twenty years.

Oft I Think of Thee

Oft I think of thee
together as one, you and me—
    the fun we had,
    the love we shared.

Missed you when you went abroad
to tend to "chirren" missing mom—
    we vowed to stay in touch,
    we planned that I would follow soon.

When death came and seized
the very breath of all—
    I felt my life was at its end,
    I had no reason to carry on.

As time slipped by the great I am
within my soul—my very being—
was helping me and guiding me
through this great despair—
    today my life is filled with peace and joy,
    today my life is filled with love …

and silently, oft I think of thee.

Guy B. Young
Murphy, OR

[Hometown] Grants Pass, OR; [DOB] June 7, 1935; [Ed] master's degree, minister, probation officer; [Hobbies] primitive artist, paint on rocks

In 1972, I became a minister at People's Temple Christian Church in San Francisco, CA where I met and married Christine Cobb. Her children from a previous marriage migrated to Guyana and settled in Jonestown—a jungle outpost church members built and developed over several years. Christine left for Guyana in 1977. I was to follow shortly after sending our adopted daughter, Mona, in early 1978. On November 18, 1978, my family perished in the Jonestown tragedy, except for my son Joh who was with other members participating in a basketball tournament in Georgetown, the capital city.

The Son

I sat beside him in the fellowship hall,
Listened to the years of memories he recalled.
I saw the teardrops form within his eyes,
For you see he has just told Mama his last goodbyes.

I watched him walk with a heavy heart,
As he returned to the graveside plot,
And I in the shadows did as I best thought,
To Heaven an arrow prayer I shot.

Upon this arrow I attached the note,
Though silently sent, hasty it went.
A prayer for strength much like a coat,
For you see that God's word gives hope.

And though the hour it be late,
The "Master" bricklayer mansions He's still building,
So until it's done, "Wait upon the Lord."
For He will renew your strength
That you like her, will mount upon eagle wings,
You son, will walk and not faint.
For now all you must do is wait.

Wait means to remain in readiness to serve Him.

Frank A. Patterson
Culleoka, TN

[Hometown] Culleoka, TN; [DOB] August 25, 1941; [Ed] high school, airline/security; [Occ] retired US Airways (RRS) supervisor; [Hobbies] Bible reading, writing, and walking; [GA] poetry published

I am a retired RRS (Ramp Service Supervisor) For US Airways. A widower, I enjoy writing as God gives me the words to write. The scene for the poem "The Son" was our church fellowship hall after the funeral of Sue Baker (pastor's grandmother). As I sat and watched her son, God gave me this poem. As I often tell people who ask, God writes my poems, I only put them down on paper.

For the Win

I almost lost my chance
I practically let it slip
But at the last second I changed my mind
I gathered my strength and tightened my grip
I hit it hard and fast
I was bruised, battered, and breathless
But I held on tight
To lose was not an option
I kept moving forward even though there was no end in sight
You see the worst battle is not what you think
It is void of scratches, scars, and screams
It happens the moment you find yourself standing on the brink
The battle is with yourself
The war of course as well
The battle cry rings out in that moment
The moment you open your eyes
You have to believe you can do it
No matter what it is
For only you can start it
And finish for the win

Lauren Franklin
Orleans, MA

Catch a Falling Star

Stake a leaning tree
Which gave to many shade
Tasty fruit and rest, and
So many friends has it made.

Cheer a little child who
Is lost and wants his mother—
For to him, she gives more
Comfort that any other.

Feed a little bird
And for you it will sing
Or squawk or chirp before
it takes off on the wing.
Lift a fallen hero and
Thank God for his giving
Because of him or her
We are still living.

Catch a falling star
And polish it so bright
That it will sparkle
Gleam and shine with
Everlasting light.

Maria E. Herbert
Lead, SD

[Hometown] Lead, SD; [DOB] August 12, 1931; [Ed] Aquinas College; [Occ] former teacher, now retired; [Hobbies] sewing, gardening; [GA] teaching

I was born in Ranchos De Taos, NM, on August 12, 1931. My parents were Esther, my mother, and Selso, my father. I had two sisters—Aurora and Claudina—and Pat, my brother. We attended school at St. Francis and were taught by the Dominican Sisters from Michigan. It was one of those sisters, Sister Rose Imeldee who taught me in third and seventh grade and got me interested in poetry. She showed us how to make booklets and put our poems and pictures in them. I thank God for the beautiful people he has sent along my way of life.

Grandma's Friend

Heidi is my grand dog, she's tan and black
She's short on legs and long in the back
Her tummy almost touches the floor
She eats all her food and then begs for more

She doesn't gossip about when I'm not around
Or spread ugly rumors about me in town
She doesn't care if my shirt is torn,
My shoes run over, my denim's worn

She meets me at the door with a woof and a wag
She doesn't criticize and she doesn't nag
On her I know I can always depend
To be my loving loyal friend

There is no greater gift you can get anywhere
Than twenty pounds of love wrapped up in dog hair.

Wana Hempe
Hermiston, OR

[Hometown] Hermiston, OR; [DOB] March 9, 1921; [Ed] high school; [Occ] farmer, hospital housekeeper, sausage kitchen stuffer; [Hobbies] Reading, crocheting, gardening

I was born and lived all my life in La Grande, OR until four years ago I moved to Idermiston to be near family. I have lived on a farm, picked fruit, worked in a sausage kitchen, was a hospital housekeeper, and a grocery clerk. I am ninety-two years old and enjoy writing these little verses to keep my mind from going kerplap with the rest of my body. I love to crochet, read and garden, but can no longer see to do that.

Where Are You?

"Where are you?" I call into your study.
Your monitor is dark, your desk is bare of papers,
And unread magazines pile up beside your easy chair...
                You are not there.
"Where are you?" The roses need trimming, and weeds
invade the flowers. I peek into the garden shed;
Your old straw hat sits atop your trowel and rake.
                You are not there.
"Where are you?" Your workshop is strangely quiet.
Tools lay deserted upon the bench: hammers in a row,
the electric saw covered; boards waiting your touch, but
                You are not there.
I walk down the hall to your white, sterile room—
There you are! Staring at a muted TV
I call your name...you turn to me with eyes blank as winter snow fields.
I hug you against my aching heart, but you turn away.
                You are not there!
                Where did you go?

Alice Marks
Marion, IA

I wrote this poem several years ago, but recently I have been living it. My husband, Murray, passed away in August. Our five children, scattered coast to coast, have been a wonderful support, as have hospice and residents in the retirement home here in Iowa where I live. We were married an unbelievable seventy-one years, so I feel like part of me went with him. Now I am remembering those happy days and years that motto we lived by: "Let us continue to discover, we are good for one another."

Memories of You

When your day begins, do your thoughts go to me
When we first met how things used to be
Are your thoughts of me as you walk out the door
Hurrying to work just like before
When the rain falls gently on your car as you wait
Do you remember the good times we shared
The tragic events that tore us apart
Are forever in my thoughts
Are forever in my heart
I think of you often and where you might be
Are you happy, are you angry, or sad
Do you still feel the pain of the last day we shared
Do you remember our talks, our days, do you care
My memories come crashing in on my thoughts
When I least expect them to
You have to know I loved you so
My days and world were you
I've often tried to forget that time
But this pain I feel is real
I wish I could see or talk to you
And tell you how I feel
Wherever you go
Whatever you do
All my love I send to you
Because I loved you so

Cherie Chilvers
San Bernardino, CA

[Hometown] South Haven, MI; [DOB] September 8, 1947; [Ed] high school and medical assistant; [Occ] lab assistant; [Hobbies] reading, writing poetry, and travel; [GA] giving birth to three children

Eber & Wein Publishing

Love at First Blush?

Love tripped lightly by today,
Tossed her head and smiled.
A saucy, teasing Imp at play…
A vixen, sweet and wild!

Betty Paschall Grantham
Grantham, NC

Sleep

Drowsiness comes over me
like a beautiful, broken sea—
Carries me gently
into reckless danger.
Gentle.
Sleep.

Abigail Rea
Greeneville, TN

Join Me on the Patio

Join me on the patio,
We'll see sun's final citron sparks
Before the curtain lowers
Violet curtain known as "dark."

Listen to the distant
Marsh frogs hoarsely croak and rasp—
Butterflies, crickets in dewy grass.

Oh, let us drink elixir
Of honeysuckle's yellow blooms,
Light cologne of jasmine,
Exotic spices of rose perfume.

Join me on the patio,
We'll see sun's last vermilion sparks
Before great Heaven lowers
Violet curtain known as "dark."

Marian Hallet
Los Angeles, CA

[Hometown] Rochester, NY; [DOB] March 16, 1952; [Ed] graduated from private high school, one semester of study at Manhattanville College; [Occ] homemaker, aspiring writer; [Hobbies] writing memoirs, poetry, fiction, reading; [GA] winning Editors Choice awards, having poems published by Eber & Wein Publishing and minor poetry magazines

Poetry of the Love Song

Another bride, another June
And so it goes Rosemary crooned.
The soprano high, the tenor mellow
In Italian it will bellow.
A kiss, a rose
A lyric everyone knows.
Remember it, remember forever
For it will keep us together.
Come hold me closely, make me smile
In the windy city awhile.
And if the wicked game to play
Torment follows another day.
Be strong, take stance
When caught up in bad romance.
Should I go? Should I stay?
Belt it out, just walk away.
Serenade the melody, whine, warble, or cantillate
It is ours we proclaim, paying homage to the date.
I think I love you, I think I do
These silly love songs we pay ado.
Pen another, pen one more
For it's the love song we adore.

Bonny M. Winberg
Franklin, WI

If I Believed in Angels

If I believed in angels
I'd believe that you were one
When you came into my life
I believe my heart you won

I'd been alone for a while,
Waiting for someone like you.
Then I saw your sweet, sweet smile.
When we danced 'twas then I knew.

You'd be the one to steal my heart.
Your laughter brightened my life.
Even when we were apart
I hoped I could be your wife.

It's the way you show your love
And the ways you understand,
All your gifts from God above,
And even how you hold my hand.

If I believed in angels
I'd believe that you were one.
Now that you are in my life
As man and wife we are one.

Evelyn H. Heckhaus
New Bern, NC

Living New Bern, NC my entire life, and enjoying living only forty-five minutes from the beach, gave me many opportunities to enjoy the ocean's beauty. In my seventy-six years I have attended East Carolina University and used my degree in home economics to teach for many years in the county schools. Currently I enjoy making costumes for a local dance studio, hemming projects for my friends, writing stories for children and writing poems. Many church activities keep me busy, also. I recently remarried as my first husband died a few years ago. This poem reflects my feelings for my "new" husband.

Our Secrets

Secrets, we all have them
Some are meant to be kept
Others must surely be told
Eventually…
Are we condemned to repeat
Our mistakes until we learn from them?
Do we remember the past
Or hide it?
Not everyone can accept
Our differences
And sometimes, similarities
Make us crazy
Why must we hide
Who we are?
It doesn't make sense
To live your whole life
Pretending to be
Something you're not
Especially when all you want
Is someone to love you
Just the way you are

Elaine M. Isaacson
Fredericksburg, VA

A Wise Old Friend

A very incredible man so full of laughter,
love, and life. I will remember him always and forever. Almost a century he has lived with us.
Much laughter and teasing was seen each and every day.
Love reigned strong in his heart even to the very end of his days.
Time has passed now so has he, remembering all that he did would take many years to complete.
At different times he was very special to me, and at other times I seemed very special to him.
Many cherished times we have shared that we both loved and were incredible!
Close moments are to be seen no more, never to be forgotten. He will always be talked about
 and be remembered by all he knew.

Robin Briand
Montgomery, NY

   I was blessed to find a man to marry, who is fulfilling this new generation like the old man once did.

Dreams Create

Believe in yourself
Believe in the world
When you're afraid
Close your eyes
Unleash the light that lies within
Let your dreams run wild with no end
Dream to be brave
To fight like a warrior
Hope to fly
As you soar through the sky
Be passionate, be free
A dream is divine
Because
Dreams create hope
Hope creates ambition
Ambition creates life
Life with a mission

Cassie Luton
Sand Springs, OK

[DOB] *May 29, 1994; [Hobbies] singing, games, Harry Potter, Lord of the Rings; [GA] loving life*

I believe in believing. It can all lead back to a dreamer's dream.

Happy and Sad

When I am feeling happy
I just lift up
My head
When I am feeling sad
I just get up
And look
About
Whenever I am feeling
Glad
Whenever I am feeling
Sad
I sing a song
That lets you
know I
Care.

Cherese E. Nelson
Copiague, NY

I am an alumna of the University of Massachusetts at Amherst.

Lord, Give Me a Little

Lord, give me a little bit of your time
What little I ask of you will ease my mind
For someone to trust in a faith that I know
Show me direction, which way should I go?

Life gets harder with each passing day
Things taken for granted slowly slipping away
Show me direction, which way should I go?
A message, a signal—never let go

My head is spinning, the world turns around
Searching, searching...to find sound ground
Retracing steps, mistakes that I made
Repaying favors that haven't been paid

Troubles that happen when things go awry
With lovers or friendship, tears in my eye
Show me the strength that I have within
I'd like to start over, let beginning begin

Love seems to die as it lays on the vine
Though love is everything, God's great, divine
Strengthen my heart, and strengthen my soul
Show me direction—which way should I go?

Darryl Ehlers
Lynden, WA

I am a fourth-generation farmer who lives his life by Christian rules. I have been a farmer all of my life and am making history a reality. I hardly ever read a book the whole way through; however, I love writing. It gives me wisdom, similar to snapping a picture. A poem to me is a picture in words.

I Shudder

Thoughts of you running around
    in the privacy of my mind
  Finding their way to visions in kind
  Emotions deep, dark grip me
  Living in the stark nakedness of reality
  Your power overwhelms insanity.
      I shudder!

Halina Ré
York, PA

Torn away from their parents during WWII, the new parents and their little girl came to America on 09/11/49. New life, new language and customs to learn. I, the little girl am still on the journey of learning.

Christmas Lesson from A to Z

As Christmas time comes into view,
Behold my holiday greetings to you!
Carry a candle and let your love glow.
Detach from all stress and worldly woe.
Enjoy some eggnog, a hot toddy or two.
Feel happy each morning—whatever you do!
Go take on your day with a little prayer;
Happy to know how much God really cares.
Imagine the sunshine in case it's asleep.
Just wiggle your nose and down the stairs do creep!
Keep an eye on your gas gauge; be not afraid.
Level your spending to match what you're paid.
Manifest your loved ones, where ever they may be,
Never forgetting how to set them all free.
Organize your workload, lighten up a while.
Pluck a smile in your heart and always be in style!
Quicken your heartbeat, keep well and strong.
Run safely and keep moving right along.
Stretch for a moment, stand proud and tall.
Take nothing for granted, we're human after all.
Unpack any luggage, unload any doubt.
Vanity is something we can all do without!
Widen your horizons, be wise, warm, and kind.
X-press your ideas honestly and keep an open mind.
Yodel in the shower, yawn when you can.
Zoom into a stable... Merry Christmas my good man!

Barbara J. Ravanelli
Milwaukee, WI

We need to add poetry to the list of our senses of sight, sound, taste, smell, touch and intuition. We should also pay proper tribute to our pens, keyboards, and typewriters, etc. Or...is it really magic that marks moments in our hearts and souls? Sometimes I revert to the simple days of learning my ABCs. Life tosses us trials and try-alls from so many directions. I find comfort and joy in growing up with every season. Trying to make sense of our "whurld" is such a challenge, don't you think?

I Become a Child at Christmastime

Family gathered 'round the fireplace
As we listened to grandpa read the story of Christ's birth.
Outside the world is covered in snow,
Lights on the tree,
Packages wrapped in beautiful paper and tied with gorgeous bows.
The excitement of seeing Santa at the mall
Reminds me of when I was quite small.
Children finally in bed excited for Christmas Day,
Waiting for the sound of reindeer on the roof.
I believed in them then, though there was no proof.
Carolers up and down the street,
Peppermint candy stuck inside an orange;
How sweet it made the nectar.
Ribbon candy sweet as could be,
No wonder I become a child at Christmastime.

Kathy Paschal
Salt Lake City, UT

I truly love Christmastime and look forward to it every year. It is my favorite holiday. To this day I have to admit I get excited on Christmas Eve.

A Guiding Light

Within the pathway leading farther on,
There is a guiding light sending light rays along.
We may only view one step ahead.
Hold tight to instructions to be read.

A first poem written in youth many years ago
Lives on, filled with truths to be known.
Many lines have since been filled.
Lots of thought seeds have been planted and tilled.

The reader can harvest them at will.
Their message remains waiting still.
The first poem reads the same today.
It had its say and reads this way.

"Little duties done today,
Another step along life's way;
A word to help a troubled soul
Walk on toward the one great goal.

A smile to brighten a gloomy morn,
The joy to do that others may learn.
His love, His joy, His friendship is true,
Mid every storm will guide us through.

Oh! To learn more of His will today,
To have a heart, to follow His way,
To do the duty, for us He has planned,
Know the works of His mighty hand."

"Little Things Can Be Great Things"
Beneath that title its words remain.
Simple thoughts of daily life.
Find joy in things we like.

Esther Thornburg
Cantril, IA

Angels

There are many angels among us. Some are in disguise.
The woman at the grocery, the man pumping gas, and the child with bright eyes.

When things seem weary and all goes wrong and life does not seem fair,
And even in one's darkest hour there's no need for despair,

Angels will present themselves in many different ways.
And soon things will get better and you'll have much brighter days.

But believing is quite crucial. You must always keep the faith.
The power of angels is very strong—make no mistake.

Patsy Spring
Lima, OH

I was born January 1, 1954 and was raised in Leipsic, OH, but have lived in Lima for forty-two years. I have worked as a registered nurse for thirty-nine years. My hobbies include going to garage sales, volunteering for the American Cancer Society, and hunting four-leaf clovers to give them to patients, family, and friends as good luck tokens. I have helped raise over 1.5 million dollars to fight cancer through the Relay for Life. I have written over 135 poems, ninety of them for my patients, coworkers and friends. I call it poem therapy. My greatest accomplishment is that I raised two amazing children who have become even more amazing adults.

Lost Art

Cursive writing
Lost art
Controversy over should it be taught
Symmetric flowing lines
Time, dedication, perfection
Circle after circle
Stroke after stroke
Repetitive flowing, A to Z
Learning perfect ABCs
Penmanship
Painting across paper
Some are naturals
Others scribble
Like coloring outside the lines
Computers are faster
Take less time
Computers are imperative
Expressed sentiment, feelings, art
Computers take a backseat
Society has broken down
All become alike
Laziness takes over
Eliminating grace
Students of the future
Older generations, secret code
Youngsters unable to decipher
Vanishing art of rhythm in motion
By pencil
Cursive writing

Clio H. Gerbes
Canisteo, NY

[Hometown] Hornell, NY; [Occ] substitute teacher; [Hobbies] writing poetry, art; [GA] having my children and grandchildren

I live in a small town in upstate New York, from where most of my ideas for my poetry come. I thank God for all He has done for me and my family. I have been truly blessed with six grandchildren and now two great-grandchildren. Thanks to all who have read my poems. I hope some enjoyment comes from reading them!

When I Look Up

When I look to Heaven
I see beautiful clouds shining bright
And the sun shining down
But soon when I look up
I will see a smiling face shining down on me
And I will remember all the good times I've had
Because when I look up to the heavens
I will see my dad
When I'm blue I will still look to you, Dad
For guidance because I will see you shining your light
and I will know that you are with me
When I am happy, I will share those days with you too
Because when I look to Heaven
I will see you happy too
Not a day will go by without thinking of you
Because I know that you will always be there
And all I have to do is look up
And that's where I will find you
As Grandma would say when the thunder rolls
God is playing pool in Heaven
So when I hear thunder; I will know
He's playing pool with you, Dad
So no matter what I am doing here on Earth
Or no matter what you are doing in Heaven
I will see you
When I look up

Terri Whitworth
Washington, IL

[Hometown] Washington, IL; [Ed] associate's degree in marketing; [Occ] homemaker; [Hobbies] travel and exercise; [GA] my children and being published by Eber & Wein Publishing

I feel that God has given me the gift of writing and I want to share my talent with everyone. My greatest accomplishments would be getting published in Eber & Wein's poetry publications. I pray that my poems touch people's hearts as much as they do mine. My favorite poet is Robert Frost and my favorite poem is "The Road Not Taken." This poem I wrote in memory of my dad, who passed away May 29, 2013. I love you, Dad!

Benchley

Benchley is an old friend of mine
He comes to visit me from time to time
I wonder since he likes it here why doesn't he stay?
Before long, though there he goes, he's on his way
I've known Benchley for most of his life
But secretly, I also know somewhere he's got a wife
He's a real nice guy, but he squawks a lot
And I never know when or if he's coming or not
I really like him—honest, I do
The strange ones I like are kinda few
I know when he stops by here he only wants a meal
What can I do? He uses me, that I feel
He often comes by when I'm not home
And waits for me patiently, all alone
He leaves his calling cards to let me know
Some are pretty, some not so
If anyone would like a pretty souvenir and if they truly care
I've got some great blue heron feathers I'm willing to share

Adele Lafaye
Destin, FL

Don't Worry About Me

Don't worry about me—
    Because I'm not lost, but only looking
    For what will still the inner quest.

Don't worry about me—
    Because I know there is an answer out there
    That I will ultimately find.

Don't worry about me—
    Because I must travel alone and sift away the confusion
    That hides my personal truth.

Don't worry about me—
    Because I am changing into a powerful and good man
    Who will win through my efforts alone.

Don't worry about me—
    Because I stand on the shoulders of those who love me
    And who carry me unflaggingly.

Don't worry about me—
    Because my soul has grown to hold so much life
    That I will succeed with much wisdom.

Don't worry about me—
    Because I know so little now, but I'm driven to know
    What will complete my heart and soul.

So, don't worry about me.

Michael Rausin
Upland, CA

Passing Through Life

She wears her heart upon her sleeve;
As time passes by, she continues to grieve.
She thought her life would be so full;
Tears slide down her cheeks as she gathers wool.

To have been a mother a life-long best friend;
It seems these thoughts will never end.
She stands alone and asks herself why
Her entire life seems to have passed her by.

She had no vision, she had no dreams.
The fault is hers or so it seems.
She can't say when, she can't say why;
Her life's been empty, she didn't try.

What's easy for others is hard for her.
When it comes to reaching out, her mind's a blur.
As much as she wants and as much as she needs;
For someone to notice, her loneliness breeds.

She continues to gaze at the cloudy gray sky;
Begging for answers so much time has passed by.
When will she try to set herself free;
To learn to be normal, to learn to just be?

Carrie Biesiot
Albuquerque, NM

Searching

For answers
To questions
That haunt
My life

For reasons
To live, to grow
In spirit and
Mind

To believe
In yourself
In God
Who created you

To share
Your life
With family
And friends

To love and
Be loved
To give and
Receive

To trust
In His name and
The mercy
Of His love

Betty R. Patterson
Goshen, IN

[Hometown] Goshen, IN; [DOB] September 21, 1948; [Ed] Laureate certificate, Stratford Career Institute; [Occ] retired; [Hobbies] handy crafts, sewing, being outdoors

In Times Past

As I look back in time
To memories I hold dear
Of all the folks I've known
Who have given me such good cheer

I've met many good folks
Who made my life sublime
As we passed by in life
The words they spoke were kind

With their love and kindness
They kept me from despair
The times when I faced hardship
It was nice to know they cared

I have known many nice people
In days that have gone by
They must have gotten their training
From the Lord up in the sky

Though most have gone to their reward
Their memories linger on
I hope someday we'll meet again
On Heaven's golden shore

Omar A. Walker
Bluejacket, OK

[Hometown] Bluejacket, OK; [DOB] July 29, 1928; [Ed] high school, welding, mechanical, agriculture; [Occ] operating engineer; [Hobbies] singing in churches and nursing homes; [GA] accepting Christ, becoming an ordained deacon

I've reached the age of eighty-five with God so good and true, helping me live my life in ways that I should do.

Trust

How like a flower is trust.
   Fragile as a petal,
The gentle drops of trust,
   Rain down upon us.
Soak in the strength,
That only trust can give.
Walk the path of life.
Know that you are not alone.
   The storms will come.
   The storms will pass.
And in the end you will know.
   In this place, the strength of trust
      Is as great as one grain of peace.
Easy is not the path of trust.
To place our trust is difficult,
     For we know mankind, filled
    With thoughts of selfish gain,
    Desires of self-desecration,
        Place your trust wisely, do not be afraid.
      Fear will crush your will.
        Trust will raise you up.
    Trust is our only answer,
      Trust wisely!

Florence Compher
Wartburg, TN

[DOB] December 3, 1950; [Ed] AA degree; [Occ] retired; [Hobbies] singing; [GA] to love not hate

Futility

I never knew ...
how much could hang
in the balance
of indecision.

You curse me for my methods
though offer nothing new.
And now I've hit the wall
against what else could be given.

Your boyish charm has faded
to a deeper shade of blue.
Our rowboat, once so stable,
somehow lost its beacon.

It's with tearful eyes I watch
as the waves slowly overtake you.
I hope you know how much I wanted
all to be forgiven.

Emily Kavanagh
Vineyard Haven, MA

Redemptive Lord

Since time began man was created to have fellowship with God; his maker, the master craftsman, the Lord Jesus. He planted a garden, placed man in it to dress and to keep it.
In the cool of the day, Adam would talk and fellowship with God, the Lord knowing His presence. Adam named all the animals in the garden, this Garden of Eden.
God saw there was no suitable helpmate for Adam, so God proceeded to form and shape Eve, making her from one of Adam's ribs. God had performed surgery on Adam and caused him to fall into a deep sleep. Awakening he saw his lovely creature Eve.
For she would take place at his side, for she was taken out of man.
Eve would become mother of all living. For a time Adam and Eve would in the cool of the day know His presence.
Then tragedy struck. Having been told they could partake of fruit of the trees, all but one; Eve first succumbed.
Then she gave to Adam who was with her and he partook as well.

Ann Mae Roberts
Fryeburg, ME

Ann Mae Roberts is a licensed and ordained minister of the full Gospel. She is a musician, singer, and nurse. Being single and loving life and people, Ann comes from Fryeburg, ME. What is this thing called love?

Broken

God has helped me to see you for who you really are
You do not belong to me, not in this lifetime
What Satan has intended, my *God* has turned around
So, I do understand—"Do you understand *"Why?"*

A miracle will happen
A divine healing that *God* says I'm entitled to

1) The force of forgiveness
2) To forgive those who have done you wrong
3) The force of *faith* is now
4) To have *hope* no games are played; no *lies*
5) *God* will bless me and my comings and goings
6) Faith will change my circumstance
7) The force of a seed I didn't anticipate

God says to forgive you for all the harm
You've inflicted to my body and my mind

"Forgiveness" for these broken arms

Take me to the *King*
I loved and I lost
How will this life be without him?

For he who gave me—may he rot in *Hades*
That's where all those *liars belong.*

Shirley Cherokee Benton
Washington, DC

He's Always There

You're having a bad day
Your nerves are shattered, too
I think I can help
Here's what you can do

Take your troubles to Jesus
For He's awake all night
Always willing to help you
So you do things right

It really is quite easy
It doesn't cost a dime
All you have to give
Is a little of your time

No matter where you are
He'll always hear your prayer
For He's the only one
To count on to be there

Violet Bennin
Shawano, WI

[Hometown] Milwaukee, WI ; [DOB] June 18, 1929; [Ed] some college; [Occ] grateful mother; [Hobbies] dancing, music; [GA] my five children

I was born in Milwaukee on June 18, 1929. We moved to Shawano, WI in 1968. My maiden name was Mikoliczak. I had some college. I had five children. My husband was Robin Hood Builders. I was his secretary, I also taught CCD, was the receptionist at Maple Lane Health Care and tutored children. My husband and I entertained in clubs for thirty-five years. I lost him five years ago. I love people, music, dancing, traveling, writing poems, and so much more. I love life and enjoy every minute of it.

A Spring Painting

The sky is bluer than blue,
the grass is green.
Spring is painting the scene
with pompous flowers and majestic trees.
In the midst, a fountain of hope rejoices.
From afar, the mountains recall.
The sky is bluer than blue.
The grass is green.
Spring is painting the scene with
blue butterflies and blue bonnets.
Nearby, a songbird tweets to me.
From afar, the sun in gold is winkin at y'all.
The sky is bluer than blue.
The grass is green.
Spring is painting a scene in plain view.
The lovely tulips.
The dazzling dews.
The sweet roses.
Spring is newer than new.
Upon this Earth freshness looms.
Each bud is groom to bloom.

Pauline E. Blagrove
San Antonio, TX

[Occ] poet, entrepreneur, inventor; [Hobbies] exercise, volunteer; [GA] being a good citizen and serving my country

I was inspired to write poems in college. This is an awesome experience for me. Writing poems has given me the opportunity to explore a new horizon...a restored moment in time attributed to the creation of "A Spring Painting."

Tiger Ray's Victory March

Purrs, purrs from ole Tiger Ray
He brings a victory from day to day
He's the best cat in the world
He'll bring you a bird, rat, a mouse,
Or a squirrel.

He's always faithful, he's always true,
I love my tiger and he loves me, too.
As I go along each day
I'll find a victory with my Tiger Ray.

Purrs, purrs from ole Tiger Ray
He brings a victory from day to day
He's the best cat and best friend
He's faithful and loyal to the
Very end.

He's always loving, brave and so bold,
His coat is orange with eyes of pure gold,
And as you go along each day
You'll find a victory with your Tiger Ray.

Stephen Williams
Tulsa, OK

Math is my natural talent. I taught math at age eleven. At thirteen, I won a chess trophy. I made the world's largest unofficial magic math square at fourteen. I won three trophies for poems about Tiger Ray. This will be the seventh book for Tiger Ray, two of which went international. I earned a doctor of naturopathy certificate.

A Leap of Faith

The sun's last flicker
Surrenders upon the horizon's edge,
Absorbing golden auburn rays,
Fade into the darkened shadowed ledge.

While the glistening tiny starlights
Dance off the water's top
Softly sighing brings my heart to a stop.
With each breath slowly inhaling,
The misty sea air.
If life could always be simple,
without a care.

Erasing all troubles from the corners of my mind,
Thoughts of you seep through,
The cracks let two hearts bind,
The days and nights are long without you,
Anticipation eludes our next encounter, without fear.
To leap with profound emotions,
Who would have thought such a sincere notion.
A love that's honest safe and true,
A love everlasting brings and a new.
A thought of you can color my dreams;
A thought of you lights the dawning, beams,
An outreached hand, a touch of the face,
Brings comfort and safety in endless space.

Carol Scarofile Krouse
Orange, MA

The Snow Queen

The Snow Queen happily dances
on Father Winter's frosty airs.
She spins and twirls and prances
and the gift of snow she shares.
Falling, fluttering ever so lightly
softly settling upon the land.
Pure white snow sparkling brightly
gently spilling from her hand.
The Snow Queen also has her moods,
and she angrily stomps her feet,
shakes her fists, sulks and broods,
laying a blanket of snow so deep.
The Snow Queen has a sensitive side,
and if sad her tears will gush.
When with a broken heart she's cried,
she's filled the land with slush.
The Snow Queen has many forms,
some bring us joy and delight;
but she can send some awful storms
which give us quite a fright.
Like Father Winter, she won't stay.
When her work here is through,
she'll travel to lands far away;
but she'll always come back to you.

Phyllis Butler
Allenstown, NH

Mountain's Majesty

Peace and serenity envelope me,
Beauty as far as the eye can see.
The quietness of time stands still.
Echoes of the mountains
bring forth still voices
as time goes by.
The vast expanse of nothingness
only serve to enhance the beauty.
Feel the peace as it breaks the barriers
of God's majestic paintings.
Mountains so high, they touch Heaven's gate.
Open the doors of the mind
let your imagination run wild.
Be still and listen as the mountains
tell their story.
Be still and listen as
they tell of God's glory.

Dianna Yearout
Maryville, TN

I want to dedicate this poem to my brother Bob who sent me his picture of him sitting on a single peaceful mountain in a park. It made me think of how very beautiful God's artwork is, no matter where we are. Each stroke of His hand made a masterpiece across the sky for us to look at each and every day. Thank you, Bobby, for the inspiration for this poem and for inspiring me day to day. I love you.

The Brightness of Christmas

Christmas comes with
a soft, sweet glow,
with Yuletide carols
most all of us know.
Christmas is an evergreen
with blinking, winking lights.
Christmas is a snowfall
that comforts all our nights.
Christmas comes with
presents tied with ribbons bright,
and sleigh bells jingling
across the frosty night.

Bruce Mancevice
Marblehead, MA

[Hometown] Gloucester, MA; [DOB] July 27, 1945; [Ed] high school; [Occ] retired; [Hobbies] writing

Tassels Shuffling

Tassels softly shuffling,
shagging on concrete avenues
where rolling ocean whispers
Ocean Drive, SC
my kind of place!

Donald Rose
Delmont, PA

[Hometown] Mount Airy, NC; [DOB] December 23, 1938; [Ed] BS and MPA with assorted credits; [Occ] retired U.S. Navy and State Public Health; [Hobbies] Painting in water color and oils, playing Lowery organ, reading, and poetry; [GA] marrying Lovena in 1961

I grew up at the beaches of South Carolina, particularly Occari Drive, North Myrtle Beach, learned to shag dance at about age twelve or thirteen, and still love it today—got that ocean drive sand in my blood I guess. There's nothing better than shagg'n at the OP Pavillion.

Not Just a Color, but a Race

As I awaken to see another day, there are many things I have to encounter
Like mindsets in the world that still have me wonder and think, *"What is the matter?"*
It's unbelievable how life can be reduced
To a point where people are neglected and full of abuse
Society makes "color" play such a big part
To focus more on "color" than the human qualities of the heart
A color cannot defend itself and cannot thrive
A color does not move and it isn't alive
I would be doing an injustice to not even mention
That being defined by "color" has so many restrictions
It has the potential of turning great people into just a label
To feel like a stray dog eating from under a table
Diminishing a person's life to just a color is really about control
It is a political strategy that has been used from days old
It can be very demeaning to be placed in a stereotypical category
And your accomplishments as a human race be devalued, hidden, or just taken as an allegory
Just because a person may speak a different dialect
does not mean that they are not due mutual respect
Never draw back because of difficulties of not being accepted
Don't let people's perceptions of "color" keep you from the direction in life that you are headed
If you stand and look in the mirror you should be able to see
A dignified character of royalty that dwells within and all around me
Now that I know who I am I refuse to be treated like I need to be put in my place
Because I am more than just a color; I am defined most definitely as a race

James Stell III
San Angelo, TX

A Soldier's Letter to His Wife

When the letter came from Uncle Sam
 We both knew I was going to leave
I had to serve because of who I am
 Promise me you won't grieve

Our wedding night
 Your gift of innocence is remembered
That wonderful night
 When you completely surrendered

In my dreams
 Will be the taste and feel of you
From those dreams
 Know how much I love you

The times we shared
 I will always savor
Think of those times shared
 For me as a favor

The Lord be with us
 Through this difficult time
The Lord guide us
 And be ever so kind

When I left
 I was crying inside
My dear bride
 It was difficult to hide.

Fran Williams
Temecula, CA

[Hometown] Connecticut; [DOB] June 11, 1929; [Ed] college; [Occ] author, poet, and chemist; [Hobbies] writing; [GA] two poetry books

A letter from my husband in the Korean War ... it touched my heart.

That Cross

She walks around with her arms crossed.
Whereas I walk around wearing my cross.
That cross is more than a necklace to me.
Keeping your own guard up and your heart closed can only protect but it'll never help that
girl
Who was once just like you.
Do you remember when every day
You walked around with your arms crossed?
It wasn't fair.
Nothing about life was fair.
But she took the time to invest in me.
Do you know what I remember about her?
I remember her as the girl who used to wear a cross around her neck.
I remember the day she met the girl who walked around with her arms crossed.
I remember the words she spoke to me as she put that cross around my neck.
She told me now someday you'll meet a girl who walks around with her arms crossed and
pass along to her this cross because life's not fair.
You'll look into her broken eyes and tell her "Life's not fair because fairness died on the cross"
Life may not be fair, but because a Lord and Savior died on that cross
there's hope and healing for all the lost.

Stephanie Attanasio
Franklin, TN

The saying "life's not fair" always drove me crazy. Obviously life's not fair. If life were fair you would get exactly what you deserve. It is because and only because that by the grace of God and through the love of a Savior we don't have to get what we deserve. We get life instead of death, love instead of hate. There is someone who loves and holds you no matter what the circumstances are. He never leaves you nor forsakes you. He even lay down His perfect and blameless life for you. Life's not fair and that's because fairness died on the cross. That wasn't fair at all but that is the true and unconditional love of our Savior Jesus Christ.

A Freezing Summer's Day

Come back and rescue me in your Sunday shoes and collar shirts,
You fill me with lovely pleasure and never-ending hurt.
So many feelings I will contain for you until the finish,
But where did we start?
Love and resentment from your eyes shoot
Like arrows slicing my heart.
It's a cold world baby,
But I will continue to burn.
I could never conceal my flaming heart,
So now how cold can it turn?
Your bittersweet magic you always will share,
Where no other Utopia can ever compare.
Your love is a freezing summer's day,
Disease and its cure.
Love's ending always blood soaked,
But its origin always pure.

Whitney Stevens
Jacksboro, TN

Virginia the Riveter and Other Women of Strength

I found out how to succeed:
Put on a blue shirt,
That's all you need.
Don't forget to roll up…
Don't forget to roll up the sleeves.

Show them—bah, bah, bah—your muscle,
Eyeliner, lipstick,
Get out there and hustle!
Arm & Hammer mama,
Arm & Hammer mama blues!

Hot damn, cold beers!
Pepperoni sandwiches
Comin' out my ears.
Whoa! Slow down,
Arm & Hammer mama blues!

Put on a scarf that's red,
Get attention…using your head.
Keep on workin', workin' 'til you're dead.
Have fun after work.
Lucky for me, I have two blue shirts.
Arm & Hammer mama,
Arm & Hammer mama blues.

Phyllis B. Walker
Athens, TX

[Hometown] Athens, TX; [DOB] August 25, 1967; [Ed] English literature, teaching; [Occ] English teacher; [Hobbies] collecting gnomes; [GA] family

Magic Moments

Our moments are so magic,
For infinite possibilities
to reshape our lives can appear
To not take advantage of
the moment is tragic
Magic moments lie in the
transformative power of
work and play.
These events swirl around us
To drive us to ecstasy or dismay
We are caught up in the
magic of our moments replayed.

Robert A. Calhoun
Philadelphia, PA

[Hometown] Philadelphia, PA; [DOB] March 5, 1949; [Ed] community college; [Occ] municipal guard, and printer; [Hobbies] fishing, reading, bird watching, and writing poetry; [GA] having my poetry published

Recompense

As pertinacious as the breath of life
Yet consistent as a dull-bladed knife

It's like waking up on an old picket fence
Still dreaming nightmarish visions, that borderline nonsense.

Seeing logic transformed into a mirrored sequence
Reflecting images of your past and present tense
All conjured up, currently, in everyday events

These modern, made-up, metaphoric imaginations are rife
It's the retinue of reality that will rival our strife

Revealing resourceful confirmations in aspirations of eloquence
Enamored with ambiguity setting up the highest of precedence

Is it vindication or validation, or just a personal preference?
Shallow importunity, offered up as the last line of defense...

Perverting yet another doctrine, Satan, get thee hence!

Jeffrey L. White
Elkhorn, WI

[Hometown] Elkhorn, WI; [DOB] September 4, 1952; [Ed] high school graduate; [Occ] truck driver; [Hobbies] golfing, rollerblading, swimming; [GA] being a Green Bay Packer for five weeks

The inspiration for "Recompense" is Matthew 7:2.

Our Rock

Daddy
It gets hard
to watch you slip away.
I'll miss you,
but only every other day.
Because the other day
I'll be thankful
that you were in my life.
Your steadfastness
will be carried on
through your children,
grandchildren,
great-grandchildren.
We will miss you
like the tree misses the rock.
The stone may have been moved but the impression remains.
Forever it shall fill with water
till the story no longer remains.

Teresa Painter
Perry, IA

[Hometown] Lake City, IA; [DOB] August 29, 1963; [Ed] Iowa Central Community College; [Occ] nursing; [Hobbies] crafting, hiking, reading, gardening; [GA] two previous poems published

I am a mother of two and grandmother of five boys. I have been a nurse for thirty years. I have written poems since I was a young girl. I am the family historian and storyteller. I have written a few stories for my grandchildren. This poem was written for my father as I sat beside him while he passed.

Blessings

Blessings come big and small
Given by God to one and all

Count those blessings daily
Shout them out for others to enjoy

Do good in your life inside and out
that's why God sends blessings so you can shout

Your blessings may be private
But they can stir a sensation in your heart

Do not be ashamed to share
For many others really do care

When we can say, "I know that I know that I know"
Jesus truly does live in our hearts

A song says "count your blessings, count them every one"
So treasure all your blessings and hold them in your heart

Judith Heck
Wilkesboro, NC

[Hometown] Wilkesboro, NC; [DOB] June 28, 1939; [Ed] college associate's degree; [Occ] retired registered nurse; [Hobbies] reading and writing poetry; [GA] becoming a college honor graduate at age forty-one.

I am a seventy-four-year-old retired nurse who is a Pennsylvania transplant to North Carolina from Hanover, PA. I have been dabbling in poetry since the early 1970s. I am someone who has to see, hear, or feel a poem working inside for it to give me the words. The inspiration for this poem came after a lady in my church sang "Count Your Blessings" with such great force that my whole being stirred inside and gave me these words. So I say, "What a great God we serve."

My Forever Friend

I went to the humane society to see what they had,
I needed a friend, and someone I could love and
would love me back.
When I went in and I looked around,
I saw a beautiful cat lying in a cage.
I went over to him, and he looked at me with big blue eyes
that seemed they were looking straight through me.
I guess it was love at first sight, especially for me.
I went to the lady who was in charge and said to her,
that cat back there I'd like to take him home.
She smiled and said in a low voice that's a good choice.
I took him home and I never regretted it,
he was a very special cat I feel that God wanted him to be with me because He knew he
needed someone special
to care for him as he would me.
He will always be my forever friend.
I hope if and when I get to Heaven he will be there waiting and watching for me.

Rosemarie Sorrels
Monaca, PA

I'm a mother of two sons and a grandmother to a beautiful granddaughter. I like poetry, been writing it off and on for years. I have been published in Eber & Wein books before. Groucho inspired me to write this poem. He was a very loving cat, a rag doll in the Siamese line. He had a mustache and a goatee. Someone ended his life by feeding him poison or putting it on the grass. This is for him.

Sit and Ponder

Am I junk or am I nothing
I am not completely sure
I begin to ponder
In the end I would rather be nothing
Nothing at all
I wouldn't have to feel
No pain, no sorrow, no tears
That would be enjoyable to say the least
But what would I enjoy, if I cannot feel
So there is no point of being nothing
Then again I could be junk
I would get recondition for existing
No matter how small
Yet what is it to exist if you're not wanted
If I was nothing I wouldn't even care
But to not care would make me non-human
Which I suppose that is what nothing is
But junk is looked down upon as trash
And I know I am better than that
Who would care if I was nothing
No one
I wouldn't be here
But I don't want to go
So I sit and ponder a little more

Moriah Reinholz
Rock Springs, WY

My name is Moriah Reinholz. I live in a small town with less than 1,300 people. I am fifteen. I'm described as "odd" or "bizarre" by others, yet I think of myself as weird and wonderful. I do relatively normal things, hang out with friends, do school work, play on the computer, and write poems. The poems I really enjoy writing make people think. As you have probably noticed the poems I write seem sad but I am a happy kid. I just like this style of poetry. One more thing, my favorite saying is "chill your biscuits!"

Office Gossip

And so they came, in bands of two
Focus on me—focus on you
To the ones of those
who follow rules
Ethic, pride, follow to strive
for growth, standards galore
So try we must
to keep the peace
Our inner strength, it runs so deep
and through the fight, our only might
is that we may sleep at night—
As morning lifts we rise to fight again
in half glass full harmony

Cindy J. Borsvold
Adrian, MI

Punch in, punch out, do your best.

Brindy

The ugliest dog I've ever seen
Stood on my porch, looked through the screen.
She wagged her tail, held up her paw,
The ugliest dog I ever saw.

She looked at me as if to say,
"Please let me in, I'm here to stay."
I shook my head, I would not sway,
"Get off my porch! Go on away!"

Now this was many years ago,
Oh, how I've learned to love her so,
She knew her place as if by law,
The prettiest dog I ever saw.

Dixie Beth Stern Talbot
Springfield, MO

Dixie Beth enjoys writing all kinds of creative materials, including children's stories, poetry, and music, which she records (singing herself). Her CD is Look and Life. *Best wishes to all co-authors in this anthology.*

New Again—For the First Time!

We all begin as a simple blank page,
We're *New*—without hate or other matter.

We're free from the clutter of passions and stuff,
That we never sense the gorging of the latter.

Now at the *Mid* having gathered nightmares and fantasies,
Our true self begins to unfold.

Memories now engulf that once blank page,
As we're hopelessly drawn by Life's mold.

Now *Old*, with very few blank spaces free,
Tell me—Is this now the true me?

Then somehow between *Old* and *Gone*—our memories are wiped and cleansed,
Someway we've been purged throughout,
For we're all blank like *New* again.

As we meet *Old Friends* for the very first time,
Our page again is blank.

For from *New* to *Mid* to Old and *Gone*,
The journey itself is the thanks!

Steve Rosenthal
Holiday, FL

There Is Beauty

There is beauty in creation
a gift from up above
Our Creator, the Almighty
has bestowed this with His love.

There is beauty in the flowers
as they bloom again each spring
and when the day is dawning
and the birds begin to sing.

There is beauty in the raindrops
as they fall upon the leaves
and when the wind is blowing
as it whispers through the trees.

There is beauty in the sunshine
as it peeks around the clouds
as in a newborn baby
when its cry is heard out loud.

There is beauty all around us
If we take the time to see
It's the blessing of creation
and it's meant for you and me.

Janice I. Sherman
Concrete, WA

[Hometown] Concrete, WA; [DOB] June 5, 1957; [Ed] high school; [Occ] caregiver; [Hobbies] writing poetry, music, and crafts; [GA] being a published poet

I live in a small country community. I am a mother of three, and grandmother of eight. I have worked as a cook, housekeeper, activity person and caregiver for the elderly. My husband and I have a small band and love entertaining the local folks. My hobbies include writing poetry, crocheting, gardening and music. I love my Creator, my family and my life.

Legacy of a Smile

Meeting a true love
    A smile of flirtation.
Confessing marriage vows with a lifelong partner
    A smile of commitment.
A colicky newborn finally falling asleep
    A smile of peacefulness.
A seven-year-old boy catching a pop-fly in right field and making a double play.
    A smile of confidence.
A creative young woman receiving an honor to the Fine Arts Academy
    A smile of success.
Donating the opportunity of a child to feed exotic animals in a small petting zoo
    A smile of curiosity.
Consoling a friend "feeling blue"
    A smile of empathy.
Offering fresh pizza to a sleeping homeless woman on the subway
    A smile, adding a praised "God bless" to the deliverer.
Pushing a stalled car for a man resembling Santa across a busy, six-lane intersection
    A smile of appreciation.
Providing a meal for a frail man counting his pennies in a hospital cafeteria
    A smile of surprise.
Opening the door for a double-amputee war vet
    A smile of pride.
Comforting a dying cancer patient with a relaxing backrub
    A smile of peace.

Trudy Eckstein
Kearney, MO

Hearing God's Voice

Will my Bible just lay there collecting more dust?
Like an abandoned car groaning in rust?
Or will I consume sacred pages that nourish the soul?
With its spiritual vitamins that make one healthy and whole
God's word assures me daily of His love and care
Therefore, my heart has no need to despair
He guides my footsteps along this perilous trek of life
And promises victory and blessing beyond my turmoil and strife
So share this Gospel with love and kindness
Throughout this world of heartache and chaos
My Savior will soon whisper gently and take hold of my hand
Until then, I'll abide in His love and follow His plan.

William H. Shuttleworth
Jacksonville, FL

[Hometown] Philadelphia, PA; [DOB] May 6, 1937; [Ed] Philadelphia College of Bible; [Occ] furniture finishing and restoration; [Hobbies] acrylic painting, photography, and travel; [GA] letting go of the past

This poetic sermonette reflects my memorable and joyful rescue mission preaching days. A youthful God-encounter nudged me towards theological training. Challenging experiences still abound in this everyday school of hard knocks. Of necessity, I acquired the skills of a furniture craftsman, which sustained me financially over the years. I've enjoyed traveling, photography, painting on canvas, and finally retirement. Within the whirlwind of all of this, my pen scrolled artistic expression through poetry. Eventually, there emerged several book titles of my own creativity. Also, over the past decade, my prickly response letters have appeared multiple times in a local tabloid. Nevertheless, my life's sole aim shall always be, "to live with eternity's values in view."

Reckless Abandon

With reckless abandon, I seek Your presence in this place
With perceptive emotion, I submit to follow Your ways
All of our days collide in time
I find Your strength in my weakness
Your faith in my brokenness
Your peace in my recklessness
For, as I found You
You sent me on a journey
I sent myself on another path
And here I still stand in the midst of the aftermath, all thanks to You
Forever in the place under Your instruction
A new creation of dedication
A blessed blessing to be a witness to share the truth of Your Love
More than I deserve
You accepted the least of me, the worst of me, the best of me, every part of me
Knowing I would become more in Your presence when I was ready
And spread Your Word to more than have heard
For all need to know Your love

Francisca Ronda
Staten Island, NY

Bridge to Paradise

One night I dreamed I took a walk
Across a stretch of ground.
The ground was covered with rotted timber,
And junk was all around.
I was passing through what seemed to be
My life of sin and shame—
But I kept on walking hopelessly,
With nothing in life to gain;
Then, just ahead I saw a bridge
Over a river sparkling blue;
And across this bridge I saw a meadow
With grass all anew.
Inside this meadow, I saw a man;
He was standing upon a hill;
His arms were reaching outward to me,
And He said, *"Peace, be still!"*
I knew not what to say to Him,
Nor, could I look upon His face,
Because I felt the presence of the Lord
And the glory of His grace.
Then I knew this was the Son of God
Because His glory was divine,
And He said to me, "Come on across to Paradise,
Thou art Mine!"

Terry Webb
Los Angeles, CA

I, Terry Webb, am the author of Poetry to God: Volume 1. Throughout my life, I've stored information collected from experiences and try in some way to make sense of it. When I am not able to fully understand the things that occur in my life, I take time to process the information. By doing this, I am afforded a different perspective, thus allowing me to think more clearly about difficult or perplexing events and emotions. Poetry is a way in which I choose to externalize my thoughts. Poetry is a very powerful tool by which I can share sometimes confusing, sometimes perfectly clear concepts and feelings with others. All I simply want is to share in poetic form something that has touched my life in some way to others. Some of my poems may speak to the hearts of certain readers more than others, but keep in mind that each poem is the voice of my mind that needs to make sense of this world, of my heart that feels the effects of every moment in this life, of my heart striving to have a closer walk with God. Visit my website at: poetrytogod.org.

Questions

Questions cloud my mind
Answers I cannot find
My head pounds, my body aches
Deep within my heart breaks
So much loss, so little gain
Perhaps finally I am insane
Or just so tired I have become
That all my feelings have gone numb.
Searching always for the light
Still lost in perpetual night
Life it seems an impossible test
A cruel hoax, an improbable quest
Yet on I strive, day after day
But why: not even God will say.

B.J. McKee
Charlotte, NC

[Hometown] Charlotte, NC; [DOB] March 17, 1954; [Ed] GED; [Occ] several depending on need; [Hobbies] arts, crafts, writing, and poetry; [GA] a forty-one-year marriage, two sons, and two grandchildren

I enjoy all forms of the creative arts and hope to encourage others who read my work to take pen in hand and follow suit. Remember that the only true failure in life is not trying!

Outpouring of Love

I reached the lonely hilltop not so long ago
Thought I'd never live to see again the sky so blue
The sunshine's embrace and summer breeze's blow
Nor hear the bird's sweet song and watch the sunset glow.

Filled with anguish, my heart aching, my soul searching
But joy came in the way like sunshine after the rain
My eight children came running
Sue, Beth, Rose, Chit, Vic, Gina, Tina and Carina
With their husbands' and wife's support unending

I have God-send gifts of their giving
They go to all extremes of loving and caring
They're generous givers, spending time, effort and means
No favor or word of praise in the asking

My loneliest days, they are always there
Tender touch, things galore they give
In unselfish myriad of ways, indeed
Love outpouring, a hope to live

How can I equal these splendid deeds
The glimpse of joy holds more than I have
My unfailing love is more than I did
Which is clearer, surer, deeper and dearer is all I can give

Luisita P. Prieto
Elmont, NY

[Hometown] Philippines; [DOB] August 19, 1924; [Ed] nursing degree; [Occ] retired registered nurse; [Hobbies] reading, writing prose/poetry; [GA] published articles and poems in local newspapers in the Philippines and in the United States by Eber & Wein Publishing, promotion from staff nurse to administrative nursing supervisor, elected three times to president of Veterans' Memorial Hospital Nurses' Association

I'm truly blessed to have my lovely children and thoughtful sons-in-law and daughter-in-law who extensively cared for me and sustained me when I was "down and out" during and after a heart surgery with serious complications just recently. This poem is heartily dedicated to them. I am grateful beyond words with my unceasing love for them.

These Hands

Crying,
hurting deep inside,
life full of emotions...
Did her mother sin?
These awful, deformed hands
to contend with all my days
sadness inside,
as others' stares and gazes
Father, can't handle
stuffing them under my arms
Don't make me show them
causes me more harm
No one to play with
with deformed hands
Hide them, hide them,
deep within the sand
Out of the sand
they're still the same
hurting, crying
all over again
Why can't I be like others,
hands of perfect form?
Until I find the answer,
They're neatly tucked under my arms.

Gladys B. Nance
Gray Court, SC

[Hometown] Gray Court, SC; [DOB] July 25, 1950; [Ed] South Carolina State University; [Occ] preacher; [Hobbies] writing, crocheting; [GA] becoming an ordained minister

This poem was written because I was born with deformed hands. It was difficult as a child, and having to deal with the stares and fear in the children's eyes of not wanting to play with me because of my hands. Therefore, I would hide my hands by keeping my arms crossed to keep them out of sight. Even though it still brings tears to my eyes when I read the poem, I know why I have these deformed hands: they are to point souls to Christ. I am married to James Nance and we have a son, Nikki D'Angelo Nance.

Senior Moment

A senior moment came and went
of that there was no doubt.
In midst of my embarrassment,
I wanted to scream and shout.
Her name, the face I clearly saw,
recognition was not there.
I smiled through my eyes dulled.
All I did was stare.
Her hand held out to mine.
I gripped it in despair.
The smile returned said it all
I know, I've been there.

Loraine Faschingbauer
Bloomer, WI

Now that I am a senior, these moments happen in many situations. I love it, really.

Hitch Hiker

Dryboned on the Plains,
a cowboy sits and shakes;
his ancient pickup flattened
in a rodeo of miscalculation.

A victim of a blown tire
(and a pint of Jim Beam),
he gets some free advice
and a fast ride to Roswell.

Out in the Mescalero Sands
a young buckaroo once again
sidesteps the Highway Patrol
—and a broken neck.

Frank M. Phelan
Tacoma, WA

Having traveled throughout the West since 1956, I've been writing cowboy poetry for decades. Now seventy-four and retired, I've found my niche along the shores of Puget Sound.

The Slumbering Rose

Within the grasp of winter's fury
snowdrifts mark their place,
stoic sentries show no hurry,
locked in cold embrace.

Encased beneath and yet unseen,
in darkness fully bound,
a thorny bush, devoid of green
rests static in the ground.

The rosebud deep inside that slumbers
yearns for spring's return,
still, the bloom that chill encumbers
feels no sense of spurn.

Instinct whispers, hold your folly,
stay away your deep despair,
lift your sense of melancholy,
days will soon be fair.

So like the rose, when hardship falls
and life will yield no bower,
know that soon with May's first call,
you find a blooming flower.

David Argier
Henderson, NV

I am a middle-aged father, grandfather and husband. I have been happily married for thirty-five years to my incredible wife, Margaret. I enjoy writing poetry because it helps me share a hidden part of myself friends and family rarely see. I tend to write from a perspective that life is beautiful, filled with both joy and pain—and must be embraced in its entirety. With that thought in mind, I am honored to have this particular work published, and it is with the humblest of hopes that it brings joy to all who read it.

Blue Skies and Sunshine America

No other land I'd rather be
that's as tropical as ours—
where waters remain blue or green
and there are lots of pretty flowers.

This is America, land that I love,
where our flag banner waves
of red, white and blue.
A country so grand and beautiful to see—
my home, sweet home, land of liberty.

We support our troops
while they go away
with prayers of hope, and dreams
they will return home, we pray.

America the beautiful, and so very free
where we can share our dreams
of Oh, yes we can...
No other land in which I'd rather be
as grand as ours alone.

A place of blue skies and sunshine
that I can call my home.
America, you're beautiful,
and you always will be!

Earnestine Smart
Palmetto, FL

He's Calling

Roses are red, violets are blue, Jesus' blood
washes through and through. Call on Him when
you're in trouble. He always comes on the
double. He loves you so and wants you to know,
He's coming back, get yourself packed.
Darkness is coming on every side, in Him you
can safely abide.
Why do you wait when you hear His call? He's
calling you to a feast and a ball. When you
say "yes" to Him you will never regret—
you will realize He paid your debt. It was
paid by the precious blood of the lamb. He
paid it for Peter, Paul, and even Sam, Henry
John, even Jane, it was paid for all, whoever came.
Rejoice, He's coming back until he does you
won't know lack. He's prepared all you need
and more beside, until He takes you
home ever to abide.

Amanda E. Dearing
Salina, KS

The Ever-Changing Scenery

Once I planted a small sapling.
Today, I linger in the shade of a tree.
Turning leaves are announcing the coming of fall
As I ponder upon the ever-changing scenery around me.

Across the way, I see a young man washing his car.
When did he get to be so tall?
It seems like yesterday he was a little boy
Jumping up and down on his bouncing ball.

I look around for little sister, Bridgette
always consumed with her Barbie dolls.
Then I realize that little girl is gone.
Bridgette has become a real, live Barbie
Texting Ken on her cellular smart phone.

The ever-changing scenery
and oncoming age can be overwhelming.
I long for time to be still and remain the same.
Recently, a former acquaintance approached me inquiring,
"You look somewhat familiar; what is your name?"

The ever-changing world
of high technology will go on;
But a higher power shall always prevail.
When it is my time to go, I am sure I will know
Regardless of the fact that I do not have e-mail.

Jane F. Bass
Smithville, TN

[Hometown] Jefferson, GA; [DOB] October 28, 1940; [Ed] high school graduate; [Occ] garment industry; [Hobbies] writing, landscaping

The Ocean's Song of Praise

Sometimes my waves wear shades of green
To praise the Lord, the King of kings.
Sometimes, I'm clothed in deepest blue
To sing His glories, ever true.
Sometimes light brown my face appears
To join the music of the spheres.
Sometimes I melt to dreamy haze
And still I sing Creator's praise.
Sometimes I'm bathed in soft moonglow
To worship God, His wonders show.
Sometimes, I look a silvery white
To sing the songs of His delight.
Sometimes my horizon's foggy mist
Declares His love and endlessness.
Sometimes clear blue against the sky
I worship Him who reigns on high.
Sometimes, my waves are dazzled bright,
Reflections of His radiant light.
Sometimes I'm blinding with the sun,
And awestruck by the Holy One.
Yet every color that I wear,
It does my Maker's joy declare,
For every time I lap the shore
I praise His name forevermore.

Joyce Keedy
Towson, MD

[Hometown] Towson, MD; [DOB] July 23, 1957; [Ed] BA in music; [Occ] private music teacher and substitute organist; [Hobbies] writing, music, painting, drawing, reading, walking, history, geography; [GA] using the gifts God gave me in music and writing to glorify His name

Lord Jesus is my Savior; I write to His glory. I wrote my first poem at age ten. My favorite topics are nature and praising God. This poem was written during my wonderful week at the ocean! I love seeing its different colors as its waves proclaim God's glory. My four published poetry books are Prelude to Eternity, Stunned by Your Glory, Symphony of Grace, *and* God Our Creator. *I was a church organist twenty-nine years. I enjoy visiting caverns and have played the Great Stalacpipe Organ in Luray Caverns, VA. I love playing musical instruments and teaching others to play them.*

A Cat's Stare

Zan and I home from work…
Sweat pouring down our faces
Blinding my eyes with sweat dots
Sprayed all over my sunshades.
Huddled in mid-room … disrobed.
Air condition not yet broken;
While scarfing down adzuki beans, broccoli, rice
We read hot mysteries lying side by side
Like steaming hot dogs as we both
Put down our books, picking up knitting …
In front of TV like two birds—twins with
Cushions beneath us sitting on the floor.
She knits a sweater preparing for winter
And I, a bell-pull with colored amethyst,
Malachite, crystals, bells, and stones—
A quiet fills the air.
Suddenly I feel eyes penetrating
Breaking my aura field I do not move…
The tingle does not pass, as
Suddenly eyes penetrating my concentration
I slowly look up … Her eyes direct at me.
A stare … she stares and does not blink;
Then I hear "I'm sorry I stare at you …"
I blink and laugh while she says,
"I feel like two cats outstaring…"

Alyx Jen
Dallas, TX

[Hometown] San Antonio, TX; [Ed] grad San Francisco Academy and University; [Occ] writing sci-fi novella; [Hobbies] currently writing sci-fi novella; [GA] taught beginners art and film at Sonoma State University, women studies program, traveled alone to Europe 1973

I attended San Francisco Academy & University in 1974, where I received an A+ on my essay for my final grade from my humanities professor. I decided I needed to write, since my words inspired such a high mark. Although I received an honors for my graduating degree at the university, I decided to do film instead. I held the First Women's Film Festival in San Francisco in the university's lecture hall with the aid of a projectionist from Canyon Cinema. The films shown included those of Barbara Hammer's short films and Kate Millett's "Three Lives." I then taught a beginning film class at Sonoma State University in their women's studies program. I had returned to the United States after traveling alone in Europe in 1973 to greater potential for women in media. In May 2013, I received a first place, Gold Medal Award and Critic's Choice Award for my poem, "Fallacy of Need." This poem is part of World Poetry Movement's Best Poets and Poems of 2012.

Girl in Purple Dress

The vision of perfection
Object of affection
 Brilliance in the eyes of beauty of Eden
Like towards Heaven's leading beacon

Lips, crimson like fire
That marks the heart and soul with burning desire
Figure to admire
But more importantly, eyes deep like ocean of sapphire

Those eyes like immortality from transcendent expanse
Awe-inspiring when they entice
They put heart in sublime trance
When fire's reflecting my visage and their soul will dance

Patrycjusz Kopec
Chicago, IL

I was born in a small town in Poland, and at the age of twelve I came to Chicago. Except for occasionally writing poetry I don't really have hobbies. When I was a child I wanted to be paleontologist or zoologist but those dreams got shattered, so I found an outlet in poetry. It does not always come easy because of English being a second language for me and aspergers disorder, which I have, but I like to think my poems are as good as any. I also believe that they are unique among others. What I like to do most is put a reader in an unusual place and show the unusual and beautiful in something seemingly mundane. It does not always work out that way, but I try. I look for inspiration in nature, cosmos, and trying to understand spirituality. I found the hard way that even if you can express spirituality it is good to have something tangible to compare it to. The problem is that is not always possible. I love nature and I think the world is a beautiful place, and we need to take care of it.

Through My Eyes

I am beautiful can't you see
My eyes are brown, my skin a dark hue
You look at me and you do not see
The woman I have come to be

I've in endured your insults and ridicule
And the names you have called me
You do not understand who I am
Or ask me what I think or feel

But one day you will have to see
The world through eyes like mine
And realize that we are of one world
And brothers under the skin

Zelma Coleman
Athens, OH

I have been writing poems since 2001 as a hobby.

One Night Stand Mistake

That one night stand lasted
      a year or more,
Then he found out! I was
      not welcome at his home anymore!
My heart was full of laughter and joy,
      we had created a precious little boy!
He couldn't or wouldn't believe that
      I was true to him,
So he left us hanging out on a limb!
      His mistake is now seven years old,
and we are still out in the cold!
      Someday he will learn, that a little
boy's love you cannot spurn!

Deena L. Carlson
Longmont, CO

[Hometown] Longmont, CO; [DOB] July 14, 1958; [Ed] high school graduate; [Occ] homemaker; [Hobbies] fixing clocks, playing piano, and sewing; [GA] kicking my drug and alcohol addictions

I am a single parent with two sons. All the experiences in my life with John and Christopher are my inspiration! Without them, the words would never come through! They are my whole life!

Index of Poets

H

Haas, Michelle 142
Hagen, Barbara 192
Hallet, Marian 245
Hamilton, Ronald R. 193
Hamlett, Michelle L. 203
Hannawell, Vickie 115
Heck, Judith 285
Heckhaus, Evelyn H. 247
Helms, Kevin E. 134
Hempe, Wana 241
Herbert, Maria E. 240
Herman, Donna 150
Hernandez, Tori A. 92
Herring, Kristi 167
Hick, Rose M. 108
Himens, Mary K. 213
Hinkle, Kenneth 228
Hoeppner, Laura 28
Holswade, Emily Fern 59
Homuth, Arvid 74
Hooks, Bernice 98
Horzepa, Darlene Ware 42
Howe, Illa C. 159
Hubbard, Latisa D. 231
Hudson, Rebecca Guiles 75

I

Insero, Doris 116
Isaacson, Elaine M. 248
Isgrig, Carolyn 6

J

James, Stanley E., II 171
Jen, Alyx 306
Jensen, Sherri B. 111
Jensen, Tina 66
Johnson, Beverley E. 176
Johnson, John W. 70
Jordan, Paul Richard 102

K

Kaufman, Carol 229
Kavanagh, Emily 266
Keedy, Joyce 305
Kenney, Richard F. 106
Knight, Jessica Lynn 125
Kopec, Patrycjusz 307
Korientz, Sami 224
Korner, Kailey 84
Krouse, Carol Scarofile 272
Krueger, Joan Williams 99
Krusos, Emily 227

L

Lafaye, Adele 260
Langley, Helena M. 198
Lapinski, Edyta G. 10
LeCompte, Patricia 173
Lemieux, Vanessa 121
Levaas, Mae 133
Libengood, Ronald L. 119
Litteral, Sara 22
Logan, Gail 51
Lorilla, Adelfa G. 189
Lovelace, R. A. 50
Luton, Cassie 250

M

Mack, Patricia J. 62
MacNeill, Jim 1
Maddox, Troy TMX 144
Mageswari, Magiah 57
Mancevice, Bruce 275
Marks, Alice 242
Martin, Ardyce 43
Mathews, Kathy A. 80
Matlin, Marvin 8
Matros, Ron 60
McBride, Gloria 69
McCarville, Shannon 110
McCoy, Dale O. 155
McDiarmid, Donna 199
McKee, B.J. 296
Melnyczenko, Christa 149

Milby, Christa 34
Minassian, Gohar 27
Minkowsky, Allan Richard 88
Moe, Nedra S. 194
Moncion, Mercedes 79
Morgan, Easter D. 41
Morgan, Loretta L. 47
Morgan, Rachel Kristeen 97
Morris, Annelda Michelle 13
Murphy, Jefferson 15
Murphy, Patricia L. 186
Murrell, Marlene R. 124
Myers, Mikaela Nikole 18

N

Nance, Gladys B. 298
Nay, Courtney L. 39
Nelson, Cherese E. 251
Neufeldt, Shanissa 197
Newton, Leslie L., Jr. 174
Newton, Nicole 56
Nguyen, Vi 109
Nulle, Leonie F. 137

O

Olson, Kara S. 4
Olson, Renae A. 136
Opper, Steve 112
Ortale-Curtis, Carole 163

P

Painter, Teresa 284
Palmer, Valerie J. 234
Paschal, Kathy 255
Patterson, Betty R. 263
Patterson, Frank A. 238
Perlinger, Donald B. 117
Perry, Pamela Michelle 85
Phelan, Frank M. 300
Phengphong, Xaysouvanh 86
Pidlisny, Amanda 196
Pigram, Jo-Anne Maree 180
Porter, Martha M. 30

CPSIA information can be obtained at www.ICGtesting.com
Printed in the USA
BVOW05s1200261213

339821BV00004BD/6/P